PRACTICE - ASSESS - DIAGNOSE

180 Days of READING for Fourth Grade

Author
Margot Kinberg, Ph.D.

Contributing Author

Christine Dugan, M.A.Ed.

Publishing Credits

Dona Herweck Rice, *Editor-in-Chief*; Robin Erickson, *Production Director;* Lee Aucoin, *Creative Director;* Timothy J. Bradley, *Illustration Manager*; Conni Medina, M.A.Ed., *Editorial Director*; Sara Johnson, M.S.Ed., *Senior Editor*; Aubrie Nielsen, M.S.Ed., *Editor*; Leah Quillian, *Assistant Editor;* Grace Alba, *Designer;* Rebecca Rhodin, *Illustrator;* Janelle Bell-Martin, *Illustrator;* Stephanie Reid, *Photo Editor*; Corinne Burton, M.A.Ed., *Publisher*

Image Credits

Cover, Janelle Bell-Martin; p. 162 Newscom; p. 198 Getty images; all other images Shutterstock

Standards

Shell Education
5482 Argosy Avenue
Huntington Beach, CA 92649-1030
www.tcmpub.com/shell-education

ISBN 978-1-4258-0925-6

TABLE OF CONTENTS

INTRODUCTION AND RESEARCH

The Need for Practice

In order to be successful in today's reading classroom, students must deeply understand both concepts and procedures so that they can discuss and demonstrate their understanding. Demonstrating understanding is a process that must be continually practiced in order for students to be successful. According to Marzano, "practice has always been, and always will be, a necessary ingredient to learning procedural knowledge at a level at which students execute it independently" (2010, 83). Practice is especially important to help students apply reading comprehension strategies and word-study skills.

Understanding Assessment

In addition to providing opportunities for frequent practice, teachers must be able to assess students' comprehension and word-study skills. This is important so that teachers can adequately address students' misconceptions, build on their current understanding, and challenge them appropriately. Assessment is a long-term process that often involves careful analysis of student responses from a lesson discussion, a project, a practice sheet, or a test. When analyzing the data, it is important for teachers to reflect on how their teaching practices may have influenced students' responses and to identify those areas where additional instruction may be required. In short, the data gathered from assessments should be used to inform instruction: slow down, speed up, or reteach. This type of assessment is called *formative assessment.*

HOW TO USE THIS BOOK

180 Days of Reading for Fourth Grade offers teachers and parents a full page of daily reading comprehension and word-study practice activities for each day of the school year.

Easy to Use and Standards Based

These activities reinforce grade-level skills across a variety of reading concepts. The questions are provided as a full practice page, making them easy to prepare and implement as part of a classroom morning routine, at the beginning of each reading lesson, or as homework. The weekly focus alternates between fiction and nonfiction standards.

Every fourth-grade practice page provides questions that are tied to a reading or writing standard. Students are given the opportunity for regular practice in reading comprehension and word study, allowing them to build confidence through these quick standards-based activities.

Question	College and Career Readiness Standards
	Days 1–3
1–2	**Reading Anchor Standard 1:** *Read closely to determine what the text says explicitly and to make logical inferences from it.*
3	**Reading Foundational Skills Standard:** *Know and apply grade-level phonics and word analysis skills in decoding words.*
4–5	**Reading Anchor Standard 4:** *Interpret words and phrases as they are used in a text, including determining technical, connotative, and figurative meanings, and analyze how specific word choices shape meaning or tone* **or** **Reading Anchor Standard 6:** *Assess how point of view or purpose shapes the content and style of a text.*
	Day 4
1	**Reading Anchor Standard 10:** *Read and comprehend complex literary and informational texts independently and proficiently.*
2	**Reading Anchor Standard 6:** *Assess how point of view or purpose shapes the content and style of a text.*
3–4	**Reading Anchor Standard 1:** *Read closely to determine what the text says explicitly and to make logical inferences from it.*
5–6	**Reading Anchor Standard 2:** *Determine central ideas or themes of a text and analyze their development; summarize the key supporting details and ideas.*
	Day 5
	Writing Anchor Standard 4: *Produce clear and coherent writing in which the development, organization, and style are appropriate to task, purpose, and audience.*

HOW TO USE THIS BOOK *(cont.)*

Using the Practice Pages

Practice pages provide instruction and assessment opportunities for each day of the school year. The activities are organized into weekly themes, and teachers may wish to prepare packets of each week's practice pages for students. Days 1, 2, and 3 follow a consistent format, with a short piece of text and five corresponding items. As outlined on page 4, every item is aligned to a reading standard.

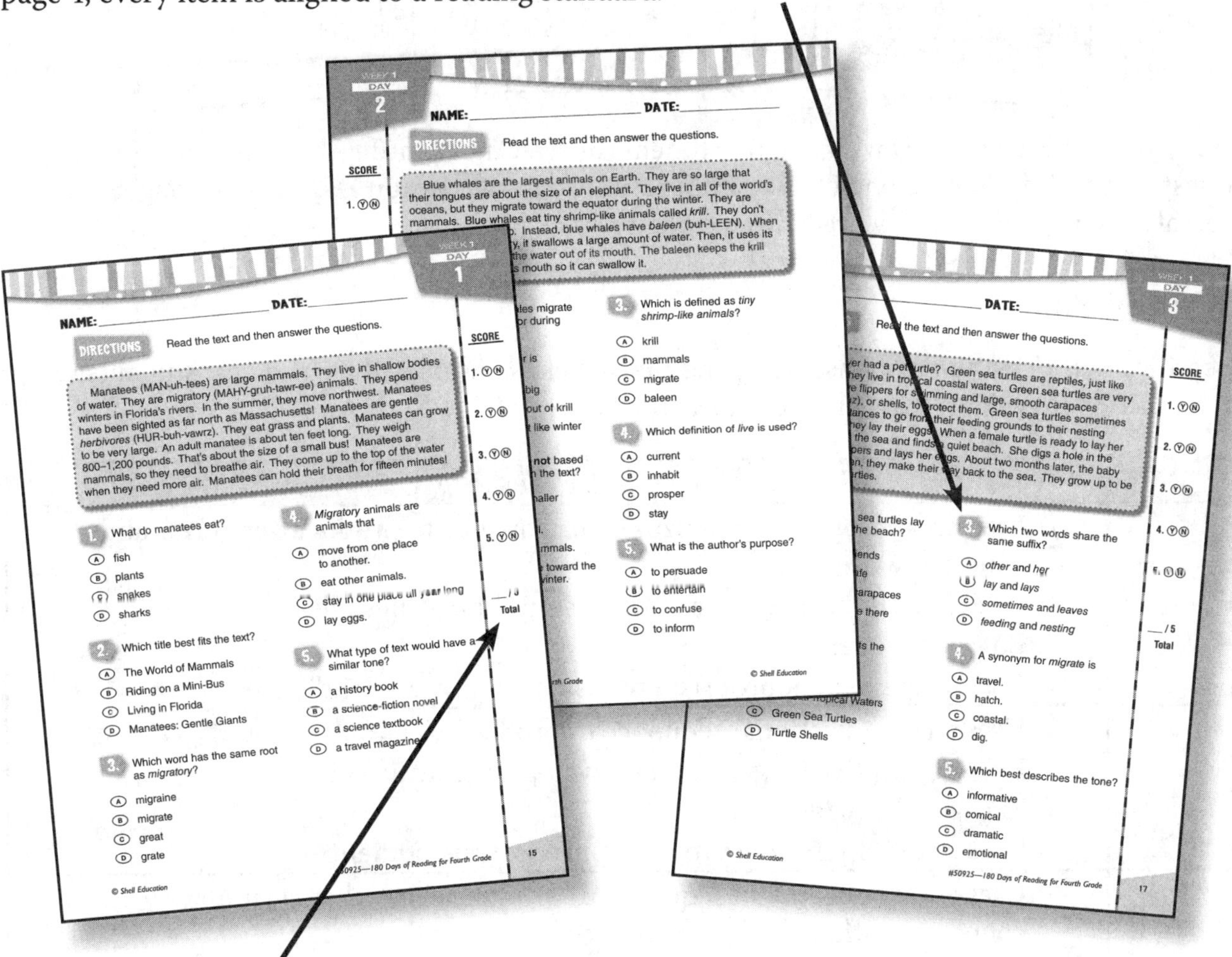

Using the Scoring Guide

Use the scoring guide along the side of each practice page to check answers and see at a glance which skills may need more reinforcement.

Fill in the appropriate circle for each problem to indicate correct (Y) or incorrect (N) responses. You might wish to indicate only incorrect responses to focus on those skills. (For example, if students consistently miss items 2 and 4, they may need additional help with those concepts as outlined in the table on page 4.) Use the answer key at the back of the book to score the problems, or you may call out answers to have students self-score or peer-score their work.

HOW TO USE THIS BOOK *(cont.)*

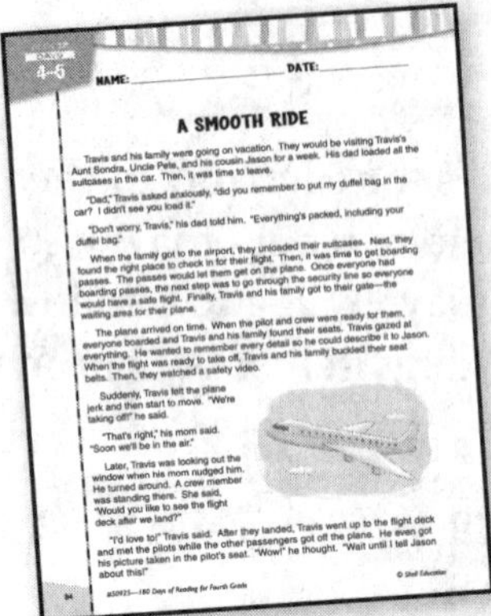

Day 4–5

NAME: ____________ DATE: ____________

A SMOOTH RIDE

Travis and his family were going on vacation. They would be visiting Travis's Aunt Sondra, Uncle Pete, and his cousin Jason for a week. His dad loaded all the suitcases in the car. Then, it was time to leave.

"Dad," Travis asked anxiously, "did you remember to put my duffel bag in the car? I didn't see you load it."

"Don't worry, Travis," his dad told him. "Everything's packed, including your duffel bag."

When the family got to the airport, they unloaded their suitcases. Next, they found the right place to check in for their flight. Then, it was time to get boarding passes. The passes would let them get on the plane. Once everyone had boarding passes, the next step was to go through the security line so everyone would have a safe flight. Finally, Travis and his family got to their gate—the waiting area for their plane.

The plane arrived on time. When the pilot and crew were ready for them, everyone boarded and Travis and his family found their seats. Travis gazed at everything. He wanted to remember every detail so he could describe it to Jason. When the flight was ready to take off, Travis and his family buckled their seat belts. Then, they watched a safety video.

Suddenly, Travis felt the plane jerk and then start to move. "We're taking off!" he said.

"That's right," his mom said. "Soon we'll be in the air."

Later, Travis was looking out the window when his mom nudged him. He turned around. A crew member was standing there. She said, "Would you like to see the flight deck after we land?"

"I'd love to!" Travis said. After they landed, Travis went up to the flight deck and met the pilots while the other passengers got off the plane. He even got his picture taken in the pilot's seat. "Wow!" he thought. "Wait until I tell Jason about this!"

84 #50925—180 Days of Reading for Fourth Grade © Shell Education

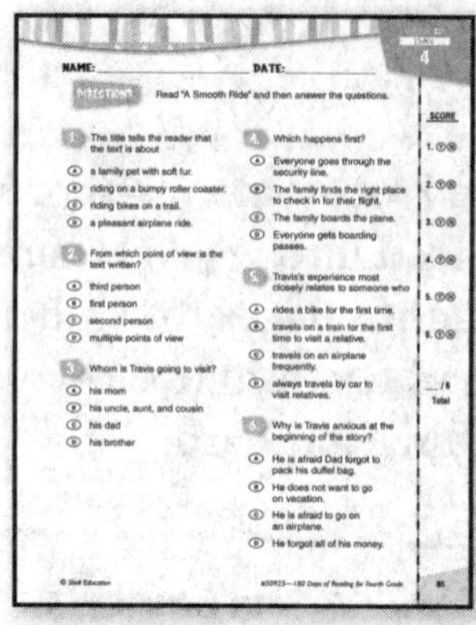

Day 4

NAME: ____________ DATE: ____________

Directions: Read "A Smooth Ride" and then answer the questions.

1. The title tells the reader that the text is about
   - Ⓐ a family pet with soft fur.
   - Ⓑ riding on a bumpy roller coaster.
   - Ⓒ riding bikes on a trail.
   - Ⓓ a pleasant airplane ride.
2. From which point of view is the text written?
   - Ⓐ third person
   - Ⓑ first person
   - Ⓒ second person
   - Ⓓ multiple points of view
3. Whom is Travis going to visit?
   - Ⓐ his mom
   - Ⓑ his uncle, aunt, and cousin
   - Ⓒ his dad
   - Ⓓ his brother
4. Which happens first?
   - Ⓐ Everyone goes through the security line.
   - Ⓑ The family finds the right place to check in for their flight.
   - Ⓒ The family boards the plane.
   - Ⓓ Everyone gets boarding passes.
5. Travis's experience most closely relates to someone who
   - Ⓐ rides a bike for the first time.
   - Ⓑ travels on a train for the first time to visit a relative.
   - Ⓒ travels on an airplane frequently.
   - Ⓓ always travels by car to visit relatives.
6. Why is Travis anxious at the beginning of the story?
   - Ⓐ He is afraid Dad forgot to pack his duffel bag.
   - Ⓑ He does not want to go on vacation.
   - Ⓒ He is afraid to go on an airplane.
   - Ⓓ He forgot all of his money.

SCORE

1. Ⓨ Ⓝ
2. Ⓨ Ⓝ
3. Ⓨ Ⓝ
4. Ⓨ Ⓝ
5. Ⓨ Ⓝ
6. Ⓨ Ⓝ

___ /6 Total

© Shell Education #50925—180 Days of Reading for Fourth Grade 85

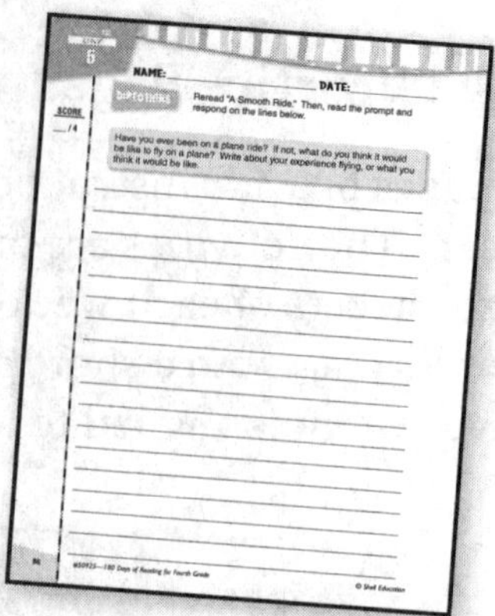

Day 5

NAME: ____________ DATE: ____________

SCORE ___ /4

Directions: Reread "A Smooth Ride." Then, read the prompt and respond on the lines below.

Have you ever been on a plane ride? If not, what do you think it would be like to fly on a plane? Write about your experience flying, or what you think it would be like.

86 #50925—180 Days of Reading for Fourth Grade © Shell Education

A longer text is used for Days 4 and 5. Students answer more in-depth comprehension questions on Day 4 and complete a written response to the text on Day 5. This longer text can also be used for fluency practice (see page 7).

Writing Rubric

Score students' written response using the rubric below. Display the rubric for students to reference as they write (G4_writing_rubric.pdf).

Points	Criteria
4	• Uses an appropriate organizational sequence to produce very clear and coherent writing • Uses descriptive language that develops or clarifies ideas • Engages the reader • Uses a style very appropriate to task, purpose, and audience
3	• Uses an organizational sequence to produce clear and coherent writing • Uses descriptive language that develops or clarifies ideas • Engages the reader • Uses a style appropriate to task, purpose, and audience
2	• Uses an organizational sequence to produce somewhat clear and coherent writing • Uses some descriptive language that develops or clarifies ideas • Engages the reader in some way • Uses a style somewhat appropriate to task, purpose, and audience
1	• Does not use an organized sequence; the writing is not clear or coherent • Uses little descriptive language to develop or clarify ideas • Does not engage the reader • Does not use a style appropriate to task, purpose, or audience
0	Offers no writing or does not respond to the assignment presented

HOW TO USE THIS BOOK *(cont.)*

Developing Students' Fluency Skills

What Is Fluency?

According to the National Reading Panel Report, there are five critical factors that are vital to effective reading instruction: phonemic awareness, phonics, fluency, vocabulary, and comprehension (2000). Rasinski (2006) defines fluency as "the ability to accurately and effortlessly decode the written words and then to give meaning to those words through appropriate phrasing and oral expression of the words." Wolf (2005) notes that the goal of developing fluency is comprehension rather than the ability to read rapidly. Becoming a fluent reader is a skill that develops gradually and requires practice. Reading text repeatedly with a different purpose each time supports the development of fluency in young children (Rasinski 2003).

Assessing Fluency

Fluent readers read accurately, with expression, and at a good pace. A Fluency Rubric along with detailed instructions for scoring and keeping oral reading records is included in the digital resources (G4_fluency.pdf).

The table below lists fluency norms by grade level (Rasinski 2003):

Student Fluency Norms Based On Words Correct Per Minute (WCPM)			
Grade	**Fall**	**Winter**	**Spring**
1	—	—	60 wcpm
2	53	78	94
3	79	93	114
4	99	112	118
5	105	118	128
6	115	132	145

HOW TO USE THIS BOOK *(cont.)*

Diagnostic Assessment

Teachers can use the practice pages as diagnostic assessments. The data analysis tools included with the book enable teachers or parents to quickly score students' work and monitor their progress. Teachers and parents can see at a glance which reading concepts or skills students may need to target in order to develop proficiency.

After students complete a practice page, grade each page using the answer key (pages 231–237). Then, complete the Practice Page Item Analysis for the appropriate day (pages 10–11) for the whole class, or the Student Item Analysis (pages 12–13) for individual students. These charts are also provided in the digital resources (filenames: G4_practicepage_analysis.pdf, G4_student_analysis.pdf). Teachers can input data into the electronic files directly on the computer, or they can print the pages and analyze students' work using paper and pencil.

To Complete the Practice Page Item Analyses:

- Write or type students' names in the far-left column. Depending on the number of students, more than one copy of the form may be needed, or you may need to add rows.
- The item numbers are included across the top of the charts. Each item correlates with the matching question number from the practice page.
- For each student, record an *X* in the column if the student has the item incorrect. If the item is correct, leave the item blank.
- Count the *X*s in each row and column and fill in the correct boxes.

To Complete the Student Item Analyses:

- Write or type the student's name on the top row. This form tracks the ongoing progress of each student, so one copy per student is necessary.
- The item numbers are included across the top of the chart. Each item correlates with the matching question number from the practice page.
- For each day, record an *X* in the column if the student has the item incorrect. If the item is correct, leave the item blank.
- Count the *X*s in each row and column and fill in the correct boxes.

HOW TO USE THIS BOOK *(cont.)*

Using the Results to Differentiate Instruction

Once results are gathered and analyzed, teachers can use the results to inform the way they differentiate instruction. The data can help determine which concepts are the most difficult for students and which need additional instructional support and continued practice. Depending on how often the practice pages are scored, results can be considered for instructional support on a daily or weekly basis.

Whole-Class Support

The results of the diagnostic analysis may show that the entire class is struggling with a particular concept or group of concepts. If these concepts have been taught in the past, this indicates that further instruction or reteaching is necessary. If these concepts have not been taught in the past, this data is a great preassessment and demonstrates that students do not have a working knowledge of the concepts. Thus, careful planning for the length of the unit(s) or lesson(s) must be considered, and extra frontloading may be required.

Small-Group or Individual Support

The results of the diagnostic analysis may show that an individual or small group of students is struggling with a particular concept or group of concepts. If these concepts have been taught in the past, this indicates that further instruction or reteaching is necessary. Consider pulling aside these students while others are working independently to instruct further on the concept(s). Teachers can also use the results to help identify individuals or groups of proficient students who are ready for enrichment or above-grade-level instruction. These students may benefit from independent learning contracts or more challenging activities. Students may also benefit from extra practice using games or computer-based resources.

Digital Resources

Reference page 239 for information about accessing the digital resources and an overview of the contents.

PRACTICE PAGE ITEM ANALYSIS DAYS 1–3

Directions: Record an *X* in cells to indicate where students have missed questions. Add up the totals. You can view the following: (1) which items were missed per student; (2) the total correct score for each student; and (3) the total number of students who missed each item.

Week: _____ Day: _____ Item #	1	2	3	4	5	# correct
Student Name						
Sample Student		X			X	3/5
# of students missing each question						

PRACTICE PAGE ITEM ANALYSIS DAYS 4–5

Directions: Record an *X* in cells to indicate where students have missed questions. Add up the totals. You can view the following: (1) which items were missed per student; (2) the total correct score for each student; and (3) the total number of students who missed each item.

Week: ______ Day: ______ Item #	1	2	3	4	5	6	# correct	Written Response
Student Name								
Sample Student		X			X	X	3/6	3
# of students missing each question								
								Written Response Average:

STUDENT ITEM ANALYSIS DAYS 1–3

Directions: Record an *X* in cells to indicate where the student has missed questions. Add up the totals. You can view the following: (1) which items the student missed; (2) the total correct score per day; and (3) the total number of times each item was missed.

Student Name: Sample Student

Item		1	2	3	4	5	# correct
Week	Day						
1	1		X			X	3/5
Total							

STUDENT ITEM ANALYSIS DAYS 4–5

Directions: Record an *X* in cells to indicate where the student has missed questions. Add up the totals. You can view the following: (1) which items the student missed; (2) the total correct score per day; and (3) the total number of times each item was missed.

Student Name: Sample Student								
	Day 4							Day 5
Item	**1**	**2**	**3**	**4**	**5**	**6**	**# correct**	**Written Response**
Week								
1		X			X	X	3/6	3
Total								
								Written Response Average:

STANDARDS CORRELATIONS

Shell Education is committed to producing educational materials that are research and standards based. In this effort, we have correlated all of our products to the academic standards of all 50 United States, the District of Columbia, the Department of Defense Dependent Schools, and all Canadian provinces.

How to Find Standards Correlations

To print a customized correlation report of this product for your state, visit our website at **www.tcmpub.com/shell-education** and follow the on-screen directions. If you require assistance in printing correlation reports, please contact Customer Service at 1-877-777-3450.

Purpose and Intent of Standards

Legislation mandates that all states adopt academic standards that identify the skills students will learn in kindergarten through grade twelve. Many states also have standards for pre-K. This same legislation sets requirements to ensure the standards are detailed and comprehensive.

Standards are designed to focus instruction and guide adoption of curricula. Standards are statements that describe the criteria necessary for students to meet specific academic goals. They define the knowledge, skills, and content students should acquire at each level. Standards are also used to develop standardized tests to evaluate students' academic progress. Teachers are required to demonstrate how their lessons meet state standards. State standards are used in the development of all our products, so educators can be assured they meet the academic requirements of each state.

College and Career Readiness

The activities in this book are aligned to the college and career readiness (CCR) standards. The chart on page 4 lists each standard that is addressed in this product.

TESOL and WIDA Standards

The activities in this book promote English language development for English language learners.

NAME: ______________________________ **DATE:** ________________

DIRECTIONS Read the text and then answer the questions.

Manatees (MAN-uh-tees) are large mammals. They live in shallow bodies of water. They are migratory (MAHY-gruh-tawr-ee) animals. They spend winters in Florida's rivers. In the summer, they move northwest. Manatees have been sighted as far north as Massachusetts! Manatees are gentle *herbivores* (HUR-buh-vawrz). They eat grass and plants. Manatees can grow to be very large. Adult manatees are about ten feet long. They weigh 800–1,200 pounds. That's about the size of a small bus! Manatees are mammals, so they need to breathe air. They come up to the top of the water when they need more air. Manatees can hold their breath for fifteen minutes!

1. What do manatees eat?

- (A) fish
- (B) plants
- (C) snakes
- (D) sharks

2. Which title best fits the text?

- (A) The World of Mammals
- (B) Riding on a Mini-Bus
- (C) Living in Florida
- (D) Manatees: Gentle Giants

3. Which word has the same root as *migratory*?

- (A) migraine
- (B) migrate
- (C) great
- (D) grate

4. *Migratory* animals are animals that

- (A) move from one place to another.
- (B) eat other animals.
- (C) stay in one place all year long.
- (D) lay eggs.

5. What type of text would have a similar tone?

- (A) a history book
- (B) a science-fiction novel
- (C) a science textbook
- (D) a travel magazine

SCORE

1. Ⓨ Ⓝ
2. Ⓨ Ⓝ
3. Ⓨ Ⓝ
4. Ⓨ Ⓝ
5. Ⓨ Ⓝ

___ / 5 Total

NAME: ______________________ **DATE:** ______________

DIRECTIONS Read the text and then answer the questions.

SCORE

1. Ⓨ Ⓝ

2. Ⓨ Ⓝ

3. Ⓨ Ⓝ

4. Ⓨ Ⓝ

5. Ⓨ Ⓝ

___ / 5

Total

Blue whales are the largest animals on Earth. They are so large that their tongues are about the size of an elephant. They live in all of the world's oceans, but they migrate toward the equator during the winter. They are mammals. Blue whales eat tiny shrimp-like animals called *krill*. They don't have teeth like you do. Instead, blue whales have *baleen* (buh-LEEN). When a blue whale is hungry, it swallows a large amount of water. Then, it uses its huge tongue to force the water out of its mouth. The baleen keeps the krill inside the blue whale's mouth so it can swallow it.

1. Why do blue whales migrate toward the equator during the winter?

Ⓐ because the water is warmer there

Ⓑ because they are big

Ⓒ because they run out of krill

Ⓓ because they don't like winter

2. Which sentence is **not** based on information from the text?

Ⓐ Blue whales are smaller than elephants.

Ⓑ Blue whales eat krill.

Ⓒ Blue whales are mammals.

Ⓓ Blue whales migrate toward the equator during the winter.

3. What does the suffix *–est* in the word *largest* mean?

Ⓐ the most

Ⓑ the least

Ⓒ already happened

Ⓓ belonging to

4. Which definition of *live* is used?

Ⓐ current

Ⓑ inhabit

Ⓒ prosper

Ⓓ stay

5. What is the author's purpose?

Ⓐ to persuade

Ⓑ to entertain

Ⓒ to confuse

Ⓓ to inform

NAME: ______________________ **DATE:** ______________

DIRECTIONS Read the text and then answer the questions.

Have you ever had a pet turtle? Green sea turtles are reptiles, just like other turtles. They live in tropical coastal waters. Green sea turtles are very large. They have flippers for swimming and large, smooth carapaces (KAR-uh-peys-uz), or shells, to protect them. Green sea turtles sometimes migrate long distances to go from their feeding grounds to their nesting grounds where they lay their eggs. When a female turtle is ready to lay her eggs, she leaves the sea and finds a quiet beach. She digs a hole in the sand with her flippers and lays her eggs. About two months later, the baby turtles hatch. Then, they make their way back to the sea. They grow up to be adult green sea turtles.

1. Why do green sea turtles lay their eggs on the beach?

- (A) so they have friends
- (B) to keep them safe
- (C) to protect their carapaces
- (D) because they live there

2. Which title best fits the main idea?

- (A) Turtle Eggs
- (B) Coastal Tropical Waters
- (C) Green Sea Turtles
- (D) Turtle Shells

3. Which two words share the same suffix?

- (A) *other* and *her*
- (B) *lay* and *lays*
- (C) *sometimes* and *leaves*
- (D) *feeding* and *nesting*

4. A synonym for *migrate* is

- (A) travel.
- (B) hatch.
- (C) coastal.
- (D) dig.

5. Which best describes the tone?

- (A) informative
- (B) comical
- (C) dramatic
- (D) emotional

SCORE

1. (Y)(N)

2. (Y)(N)

3. (Y)(N)

4. (Y)(N)

5. (Y)(N)

___ / 5 Total

NAME: ______________________ **DATE:** ______________

A WORLD UNDER THE WATER

Do you know how to swim? Some animals know how to swim from the time they are born. They live underwater.

Manatees live underwater. Manatees are gentle animals, but they are big. They can grow up to thirteen feet long. That's a lot of animal! Manatees are mammals and are related to elephants, but they do not have trunks. Manatees have flippers. They also have flat tails. Their flippers and tails help them move in the water. Manatees are in danger of being hurt or killed by boats.

Blue whales live under the water, too. Blue whales are the largest animals on Earth. An adult blue whale is about the size of a Boeing 737 airplane! They are mammals. Blue whales eat a kind of shrimp called *krill*. When a blue whale is ready to eat, it swallows a lot of water. Then, it pushes that water out of its mouth with its huge tongue. The krill stay in the whale's mouth. Then, the whale can swallow the krill. Blue whales were hunted for a long time and almost became extinct. People used whale oil for cooking, for lamps, and for other things. They used whalebone because it was light but strong. Finally, laws were made to protect blue whales. Now, most countries do not allow blue whale hunting.

Green sea turtles live underwater, too. But they are not mammals. Green sea turtles are reptiles. They live in warm coastal waters. Green sea turtles eat plants that grow underwater. Some green sea turtles come out of the water to warm up on dry land. Female green sea turtles also come out of the water to lay their eggs. When the babies are born, they make their way back to the sea. Later, those turtles will have babies of their own. Green sea turtles are killed for their meat and their eggs. Green sea turtles can also be hurt by boats and fishing nets.

Manatees, blue whales, and green sea turtles are all wonderful sea animals. We need to keep them safe.

blue whales

NAME: ______________________________ **DATE:** ________________

DIRECTIONS Read "A World Under the Water" and then answer the questions.

SCORE

1. Ⓨ Ⓝ
2. Ⓨ Ⓝ
3. Ⓨ Ⓝ
4. Ⓨ Ⓝ
5. Ⓨ Ⓝ
6. Ⓨ Ⓝ

___ / 6
Total

1. Which is biggest?

Ⓐ a manatee
Ⓑ a blue whale
Ⓒ a green sea turtle
Ⓓ krill

2. The author most likely wrote the text to

Ⓐ tell about animals that live underwater.
Ⓑ get you to go swimming.
Ⓒ tell how to catch a manatee.
Ⓓ tell about ocean plant life.

3. Which keywords are most important to the text?

Ⓐ *gentle*, *flippers*, and *boats*
Ⓑ *water*, *airplane*, and *coastal*
Ⓒ *manatees*, *whales*, and *turtles*
Ⓓ *elephants*, *oil*, and *mammals*

4. How are manatees and blue whales alike?

Ⓐ They both eat krill.
Ⓑ They are both the size of a Boeing 737.
Ⓒ They are both mammals.
Ⓓ They are both related to elephants.

5. People who like ______ would probably like this text.

Ⓐ mathematics
Ⓑ art
Ⓒ science
Ⓓ music

6. Which best summarizes the text?

Ⓐ Manatees, blue whales, and green sea turtles are all sea animals. They are endangered.
Ⓑ Many animals live underwater.
Ⓒ Green sea turtles live in warm coastal areas. They lay eggs on the beach.
Ⓓ There are animals called the manatee, the blue whale, and the green sea turtle.

NAME: ______________________________ **DATE:** ____________________

DIRECTIONS Reread "A World Under the Water." Then, read the prompt and respond on the lines below.

SCORE

___ / 4

There are many actions that people can take to help protect and save manatees, blue whales, and green sea turtles. What can you do to help?

NAME: ______________________ **DATE:** ______________

DIRECTIONS Read the text and then answer the questions.

Yesterday, I found the perfect pair of sneakers waiting for me at the mall. They were green, blue, and white, with just the right pattern. I could actually hear them calling me—"Leila, Leila, Leila!"

"Mom!" I pointed at the multicolored sneakers. "Those are exactly the sneakers I need! Can I have them? Please?"

"Let's see how expensive they are and if they have your size," said Mom.

My heart broke when we saw the price tag—$100! I knew Mom would never buy them. "What am I going to do?" I moaned. "I only have $25."

1. How much are the shoes?

Ⓐ $100
Ⓑ $25
Ⓒ $125
Ⓓ $75

2. What is Leila's main problem?

Ⓐ She doesn't have enough money for the shoes she wants.
Ⓑ She can't find shoes she likes.
Ⓒ She can't find shoes in her size.
Ⓓ She is hungry.

3. The root word of *expensive* is

Ⓐ costly.
Ⓑ express.
Ⓒ expense.
Ⓓ cheap.

4. Which word indicates Leila's emotions?

Ⓐ perfect
Ⓑ moaned
Ⓒ Mom
Ⓓ actually

5. Which sentence should **not** be interpreted literally?

Ⓐ Can I have them?
Ⓑ I only have $25.
Ⓒ I knew Mom would never buy them.
Ⓓ I could actually hear them calling me—"Leila, Leila, Leila!"

SCORE

1. Ⓨ Ⓝ
2. Ⓨ Ⓝ
3. Ⓨ Ⓝ
4. Ⓨ Ⓝ
5. Ⓨ Ⓝ

___ / 5
Total

NAME: ____________________ **DATE:** ______________

DIRECTIONS Read the text and then answer the questions.

SCORE

1. Ⓨ Ⓝ
2. Ⓨ Ⓝ
3. Ⓨ Ⓝ
4. Ⓨ Ⓝ
5. Ⓨ Ⓝ

___ / 5 Total

Autumn was definitely here. The days were cooler, and the leaves were falling from the trees. I was staring out the window one afternoon, watching the leaves tumbling across our lawn, when I got an idea. I raced downstairs.

"Mom," I called into the den. "I think I know how I can earn enough money to buy those sneakers we saw at the mall!"

Mom looked up from her computer. "And how's that, Leila?"

"People want their yards clean and tidy. I can rake up leaves for them."

A smile slowly spread across Mom's face. "Now that's a good idea!"

1. The phrases *earn enough* and *rake up leaves* would help a reader predict that this text is about

Ⓐ leaving home to earn money.
Ⓑ earning money by selling rakes.
Ⓒ volunteering to rake leaves.
Ⓓ earning money by raking leaves.

2. The dialogue in the text shows that Leila

Ⓐ cannot rake leaves this autumn.
Ⓑ is disappointed that her mother won't give her money.
Ⓒ is excited about earning money.
Ⓓ does not like autumn.

3. What is the root word in *tumbling*?

Ⓐ tumble
Ⓑ tremble
Ⓒ trouble
Ⓓ topple

4. Which strategy would help a reader define *definitely*?

Ⓐ Read the text's last sentence.
Ⓑ Say the word aloud.
Ⓒ Write out the word.
Ⓓ Find the word in a dictionary.

5. Which phrase from the text is an example of alliteration?

Ⓐ *I raced downstairs*
Ⓑ *I can rake leaves!*
Ⓒ *watching the leaves*
Ⓓ *A smile slowly spread*

NAME: ______________________ **DATE:** ______________

DIRECTIONS Read the text and then answer the questions.

It took three weeks of hard work. I raked leaves until I got blisters on my hands. I bagged the leaves and put the bags by the curb for the garbage truck to pick up. I picked up trash in people's yards and put it in trash cans and recycling bins. My clothes got dirty and my shoes got muddy, but I didn't care. Each week, I added up the money I earned and saw that I was getting closer to my goal. Then, the big day finally came. After work, Mom drove me to the mall, and I marched excitedly into the shoe store. I found the sneakers I'd wanted so much and tried them on in my size. They fit perfectly! I finally had the exact sneakers I wanted!

1. Which words tell the reader most about the text?

- (A) *raked*, *money*, and *sneakers*
- (B) *work*, *day*, and *bins*
- (C) *leaves*, *blisters*, and *trash*
- (D) *three*, *truck*, and *fit*

2. What words indicate that this text takes place in the past?

- (A) *took* and *recycling*
- (B) *getting* and *finally*
- (C) *I* and *my*
- (D) *drove* and *marched*

3. Which suffix can be added to *pick* to make a new word?

- (A) *pre–*
- (B) *–ture*
- (C) *–un*
- (D) *–ed*

4. Which is a synonym for *trash*?

- (A) muddy
- (B) goal
- (C) garbage
- (D) blisters

5. Which sentence from the text expresses the narrator's enthusiasm and dedication?

- (A) I raked leaves until I got blisters on my hands.
- (B) After work, Mom drove me to the mall, and I marched excitedly into the shoe store.
- (C) My clothes got dirty and my shoes got muddy, but I didn't care.
- (D) all of the above

SCORE

1. Ⓨ Ⓝ
2. Ⓨ Ⓝ
3. Ⓨ Ⓝ
4. Ⓨ Ⓝ
5. Ⓨ Ⓝ

___ / 5
Total

NAME: ______________________________ DATE: __________________

THE GREAT SNEAKER THEFT

I couldn't wait to show my brand new sneakers to my friends at the rehearsal for the fourth-grade play. I had raked leaves and cleaned yards for three weeks to save the money to buy them, and I was really proud of them.

When practice started, our director, Mrs. Rodriguez, asked us to remove our shoes first so we wouldn't scuff up the stage. I put my sneakers carefully in my red backpack and zipped it up before joining the group.

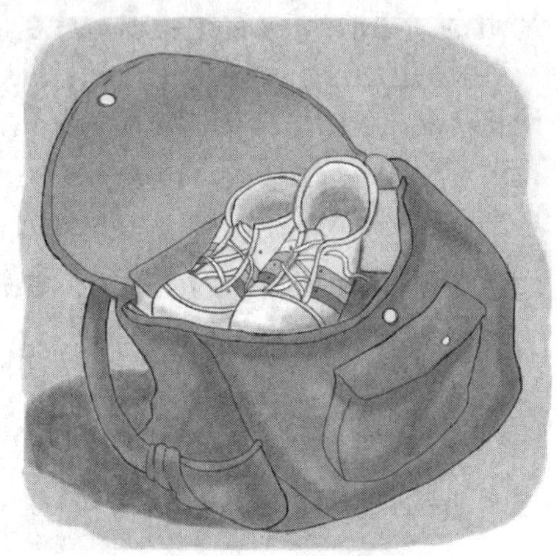

After rehearsal, I unzipped my backpack and found my sneakers were gone! I dashed across the stage.

"Mrs. Rodriguez!" I shouted. "Someone stole my sneakers! I put them right in my backpack when you told us to take off our shoes, and now they're gone!"

Mrs. Rodriguez raised her voice so everyone could hear. She asked the students to look around for my missing sneakers.

Everyone searched for the sneakers, but they weren't anywhere. Then, I noticed Sasha James opening up her backpack and looking inside. There, right on the top, were my sneakers!

"Those are my sneakers, Sasha! Why did you steal them?" I snapped.

"I didn't! I promise! I don't know how they got in my backpack," said Sasha.

All of a sudden, my face reddened as I realized what had happened. Sasha's backpack was exactly the same color as mine. I had put my sneakers in her backpack by mistake.

"I'm really sorry, Sasha. I put my sneakers in your backpack by accident. I must not have been paying attention. I shouldn't have accused you of stealing."

"It's okay," Sasha said. "They're really amazing sneakers. If they were mine, I would be upset about losing them, too."

That's the last time I'll ever say something about someone without checking first!

NAME: ______________________ DATE: ______________

DIRECTIONS Read "The Great Sneaker Theft" and then answer the questions.

1. The first sentence hints that this text is about

- Ⓐ a character who is embarrassed by his or her actions.
- Ⓑ a character who needs new shoes.
- Ⓒ a character who is anxious to show off his or her new shoes.
- Ⓓ a character who made friends because of his or her new shoes.

2. What is the purpose of the text?

- Ⓐ The text was written to entertain.
- Ⓑ The text was written to educate.
- Ⓒ The text was written to explain.
- Ⓓ The text was written to judge.

3. How does the narrator feel when she realizes she put her sneakers in the wrong backpack?

- Ⓐ excited
- Ⓑ embarrassed
- Ⓒ scared
- Ⓓ too tired

4. At the beginning of the text, the narrator is ______ to go to rehearsal. At the end of the text, she is ______ by her behavior.

- Ⓐ scared; proud
- Ⓑ too tired; excited
- Ⓒ excited; embarrassed
- Ⓓ eager; entertained

5. Which experience is most similar to the narrator's?

- Ⓐ My wallet was stolen at the museum last week.
- Ⓑ I lost my lucky pen at school.
- Ⓒ I wrongly accused my sister of stealing my shirt.
- Ⓓ I can't find my homework so I will have to do it again.

6. What lesson does the narrator learn?

- Ⓐ Other kids will take your things if you leave them around.
- Ⓑ Don't bring your sneakers to school.
- Ⓒ Don't say things about people if you don't know they're true.
- Ⓓ Never take your sneakers off.

SCORE

1. Ⓨ Ⓝ
2. Ⓨ Ⓝ
3. Ⓨ Ⓝ
4. Ⓨ Ⓝ
5. Ⓨ Ⓝ
6. Ⓨ Ⓝ

___ / 6
Total

NAME: ____________________ **DATE:** ____________________

SCORE

___ / 4

DIRECTIONS Reread "The Great Sneaker Theft." Then, read the prompt and respond on the lines below.

Do you think Sasha and Leila will be friends? Why or why not?

NAME:____________________________ **DATE:**________________

DIRECTIONS Read the text and then answer the questions.

If you're looking for a family dog, the Labrador retriever might be the dog for you. Labradors (also called *Labs*) are originally from Newfoundland. They are now popular all over the world. In fact, Labs are the most popular breed of dog in the United States! They were first bred to work with fishermen. Soon, they became skilled hunting dogs. Now, Labs are also gentle family pets. They like to be active. They also enjoy being with their families. They are smart and learn fast. Labs come in three different colors: black, chocolate, and yellow. Whichever color of Lab you choose, your Lab will be a friendly, loving pet.

1. What image would tell a reader about the text?

- (A) an image of England
- (B) an image of the United States
- (C) an image of a science lab
- (D) an image of a Labrador retriever

2. Which contains the main idea?

- (A) the second sentence
- (B) the third sentence
- (C) the fourth sentence
- (D) the last sentence

3. What is the suffix in *hunting*?

- (A) *–ing*
- (B) *hunt*
- (C) *suf–*
- (D) *hunting*

4. What color is a chocolate Lab?

- (A) black
- (B) white
- (C) spotted
- (D) brown

5. What is the author's purpose?

- (A) to entertain
- (B) to persuade
- (C) to instruct
- (D) to explain

SCORE

1. (Y)(N)
2. (Y)(N)
3. (Y)(N)
4. (Y)(N)
5. (Y)(N)

___ / 5
Total

NAME: ______________________________ **DATE:** ___________________

DIRECTIONS Read the text and then answer the questions.

SCORE

1. Ⓨ Ⓝ

2. Ⓨ Ⓝ

3. Ⓨ Ⓝ

4. Ⓨ Ⓝ

5. Ⓨ Ⓝ

___ / 5 Total

Have you ever wondered how tall dogs can get? Look no further than the Irish wolfhound. Wolfhounds are the tallest breed of dog. Their average height is between thirty-one and thirty-three inches tall—that's almost as tall as the average two-year-old human. When standing on their hind legs, wolfhounds can stretch up to seven feet! Wolfhounds are loyal to their families and are friendly with strangers. Even though they are large, Irish wolfhounds are also very good with kids. They seem to know that they have to be careful around small children. Because they're so big, they do best if they have a large yard for play.

1. How tall is the average Irish wolfhound?

- Ⓐ seven feet
- Ⓑ two years old
- Ⓒ about thirty-two inches
- Ⓓ thirty-three feet

2. Which statement is **not** true?

- Ⓐ Irish wolfhounds are very big, tall dogs.
- Ⓑ Irish wolfhounds are loyal animals.
- Ⓒ Irish wolfhounds do not need a lot of space.
- Ⓓ Irish wolfhounds are good with young children.

3. What is the suffix in the word *careful*?

- Ⓐ *–ly*
- Ⓑ *care–*
- Ⓒ *–ful*
- Ⓓ *full*

4. Which definition of *hind* is used in the text?

- Ⓐ back or rear
- Ⓑ female deer
- Ⓒ nice
- Ⓓ front

5. Which best describes the tone?

- Ⓐ serious
- Ⓑ childish
- Ⓒ informative
- Ⓓ snobbish

NAME: ______________________________ **DATE:** ________________

DIRECTIONS Read the text and then answer the questions.

If you think that all dogs bark, you haven't met the basenji (buh-SEN-jee). Basenjis were first bred in Africa. They were later brought to the United States in 1941. Basenjis have short, fine coats. They don't need a lot of grooming. They are very active, playful dogs, so they do need exercise and attention. You can train basenjis to walk on a leash and obey commands. They are intelligent and learn fast. Basenjis think for themselves, so it's important to train them early. And just because basenjis don't bark doesn't mean they don't make noise. Basenjis can squeak, whine, and even yodel!

1. Which phrase does **not** describe basenjis?

- Ⓐ *they don't make noise*
- Ⓑ *if you think*
- Ⓒ *and even yodel*
- Ⓓ *intelligent and learn fast*

2. Which title best describes the main idea?

- Ⓐ Easy Dog Grooming
- Ⓑ How to Train Your Dog
- Ⓒ Meet the Basenji
- Ⓓ The Story of Africa

3. Which word has the same root as *breed*?

- Ⓐ bread
- Ⓑ breathe
- Ⓒ bead
- Ⓓ breeding

4. What is a *yodel*?

- Ⓐ a breed of dog
- Ⓑ a toy
- Ⓒ a kind of sound
- Ⓓ a color

5. Which type of text would have a similar tone?

- Ⓐ a dictionary
- Ⓑ a joke book
- Ⓒ a fairy tale
- Ⓓ a nonfiction book about cat breeds

SCORE

1. Ⓨ Ⓝ
2. Ⓨ Ⓝ
3. Ⓨ Ⓝ
4. Ⓨ Ⓝ
5. Ⓨ Ⓝ

___ / 5 Total

NAME: ______________________ **DATE:** ______________

WHICH DOG IS RIGHT FOR YOU?

"Yes, we can get a dog." How exciting! A dog can give you several years of love and friendship. But before you bring a dog home, there are some things you need to decide. One of those things is which breed of dog to choose. Different breeds of dog are best for different families. Here are some questions to help you choose the right dog for you.

How much space do you have?

Dogs come in many different sizes, and so do homes. Make sure your home has enough space for your new friend. If you live in an apartment, a small dog, such as a pug or a Boston terrier, is a good choice. If you live in a house with plenty of space and a big backyard, you may want a large breed. Some very popular large breeds are Labrador retrievers and standard poodles.

Who is in your family?

Some dog breeds are very good with little children. The golden retriever is one of those breeds. Other breeds, such as the border collie, prefer older kids. How many kids are in your family? How old are they? Make sure the dog you choose is right for your family.

How active is your family?

All dogs need exercise, but some breeds of dogs are more active than others. Does your family like to go hiking or camping? Do you play sports? You may want an active dog. Some popular active breeds are the Irish setter and the Jack Russell terrier. If your family is less active, you will want a dog that requires less activity. Basset hounds and cocker spaniels, for example, are less active dogs.

How much time do you have?

Dogs need to be regularly trained, fed, walked, and groomed. That takes a lot of time. And dogs make good friends, so you will want to play with your dog. That takes time, too. Some breeds, such as the Pekingese, need to be groomed carefully every day. Other breeds, such as the short-legged dachshund, need a lot of training. Training and grooming take a lot of time. How much free time do you have? Will you have enough time to take care of the dog you choose?

NAME: ______________________________ **DATE:** ________________

DIRECTIONS Read "Which Dog Is Right for You?" and then answer the questions.

SCORE

1. Based on the title, which prediction about the text is most accurate?
   - (A) It is about how to correct the behavior of dogs that misbehave.
   - (B) It is about selecting a dog that best suits one's needs.
   - (C) It is about dogs from the West Coast and the East Coast.
   - (D) It is about a trip to the vet.

2. A reader would most likely read the text if he or she wanted to
   - (A) get a Basset hound.
   - (B) make sure to choose the right breed of dog for himself or herself.
   - (C) get a cat.
   - (D) get the smallest dog he or she can find.

3. Which breed of dog would **not** be a good choice if you live in an apartment?
   - (A) standard poodle
   - (B) pug
   - (C) Boston terrier
   - (D) dachshund

4. Knowing about ______ before reading would help a reader understand the text.
   - (A) dogs
   - (B) apartments
   - (C) swimming
   - (D) hiking

5. What is the main idea of the first paragraph?
   - (A) You will have to make many decisions when you get a dog.
   - (B) It is exciting to get a new dog.
   - (C) Different breeds of dogs are right for different kinds of families.
   - (D) Everyone should get a new dog.

6. Why is it important for a family to choose the right dog?
   - (A) so the family and the dog are happy
   - (B) so the family doesn't get tired walking the dog
   - (C) so the dog food isn't too expensive
   - (D) so the dog doesn't get too big

1. Ⓨ Ⓝ
2. Ⓨ Ⓝ
3. Ⓨ Ⓝ
4. Ⓨ Ⓝ
5. Ⓨ Ⓝ
6. Ⓨ Ⓝ

___ / 6
Total

NAME: ______________________ **DATE:** ______________

DIRECTIONS Reread "Which Dog Is Right for You?" Then, read the prompt and respond on the lines below.

SCORE

___ / 4

There are certain breeds of dog that are right for certain kinds of people. What kind of dog would be best for you?

NAME: ______________________ **DATE:** ______________

DIRECTIONS Read the text and then answer the questions.

"Tell Mom and Dad I'll be back at 5:00," Kyle told his sister, Jenny. "I'm going to play basketball with Matt and Sam."

"Okay, I will," Jenny said as she handed Kyle his helmet.

Kyle strapped on his helmet, dashed out the front door, and hopped onto his bike. He was in such a hurry that he turned too fast at the end of the driveway, and he tipped over and fell onto the sidewalk. Kyle slowly sat up and tried to figure out if he was injured. Everything seemed to be okay. Then, he tried to bend his arm. Ouch! Kyle knew immediately that he had badly hurt his arm.

1. What prediction is most reasonable if a reader noticed the words *hurt* and *fell*?

- (A) The text is about someone who falls and gets hurt.
- (B) The text is about someone who stubs a toe while walking.
- (C) The text is about autumn.
- (D) The text is about riding bikes.

2. What is the setting?

- (A) Kyle's room
- (B) the garage
- (C) a parking lot
- (D) Kyle's driveway

3. Which words have the same suffix?

- (A) *strapped* and *fell*
- (B) *out* and *ouch*
- (C) *told* and *turned*
- (D) *tipped* and *handed*

4. Which word indicates that Kyle is injured?

- (A) hurry
- (B) tipped
- (C) badly
- (D) Ouch!

5. Which phrase indicates that Kyle is moving too fast?

- (A) tipped over
- (B) dashed out
- (C) slowly sat up
- (D) he had badly hurt his arm

SCORE

1. Ⓨ Ⓝ
2. Ⓨ Ⓝ
3. Ⓨ Ⓝ
4. Ⓨ Ⓝ
5. Ⓨ Ⓝ

___ / 5
Total

NAME: ______________________ **DATE:** ______________

DIRECTIONS Read the text and then answer the questions.

SCORE

1. Ⓨ Ⓝ

2. Ⓨ Ⓝ

3. Ⓨ Ⓝ

4. Ⓨ Ⓝ

5. Ⓨ Ⓝ

___ / 5
Total

"A broken arm?" Kyle groaned as he entered the doctor's office. "It can't be broken! All I did was fall off my bike on the sidewalk."

"I'm very sorry," said Dr. Barlow, "but your bone is fractured. Let me show you the X-ray, we took of it."

Together, Kyle and Dr. Barlow carefully examined the X-ray. Dr. Barlow was correct; Kyle's bone was fractured. He was going to need a cast.

"This isn't fair!" Kyle moaned. "Now I can't go to baseball tryouts next week."

Dr. Barlow thought for a minute. "Is there another sport you enjoy? Maybe you could try out for something else after your arm heals."

"Maybe," Kyle said doubtfully. "I could at least think about it."

1. Which title best fits the text?

Ⓐ A Car Accident
Ⓑ A Fall from a Bike
Ⓒ A Disappointing X-ray
Ⓓ Problems with Baseball

2. What is Dr. Barlow's solution?

Ⓐ Kyle should get another X-ray.
Ⓑ Kyle should ride his bike more.
Ⓒ Kyle should try out for baseball.
Ⓓ Kyle should try another sport.

3. Which synonym for *fractured* is used in the text?

Ⓐ broken
Ⓑ bitten
Ⓒ healed
Ⓓ covered

4. Which word indicates that Kyle is upset?

Ⓐ fractured
Ⓑ groaned
Ⓒ said
Ⓓ thought

5. Which word shows that Kyle is unsure about Dr. Barlow's idea?

Ⓐ groaned
Ⓑ looked
Ⓒ doubtfully
Ⓓ examined

NAME: ______________________ **DATE:** ______________

DIRECTIONS Read the text and then answer the questions.

Kyle and Matt stood by the school gym, observing a list of sports tryout dates.

"Here's one," Matt said. "Soccer tryouts start in just four weeks, so you won't have that annoying cast on your arm by then."

"I don't really enjoy soccer," Kyle said. "Let's see if anything else seems interesting." Then, he noticed another sign—swim team tryouts! Matt saw the sign, too.

"You like to swim, Kyle," Matt said. "You should try out for the swim team."

"Maybe I will," Kyle replied with interest. "Tryouts aren't until next month."

1. How does Kyle feel about soccer?

- Ⓐ He thinks it is fun.
- Ⓑ He wants to try out for the team.
- Ⓒ He doesn't like it.
- Ⓓ He doesn't want to play the same sport as Matt.

2. What is Kyle's solution?

- Ⓐ Kyle loves soccer, so he will try out for the soccer team.
- Ⓑ Kyle can try out for the swim team after he gets his cast off.
- Ⓒ Kyle doesn't like to swim.
- Ⓓ Kyle doesn't want to play any sports.

3. Which is the root word in *replied*?

- Ⓐ ply
- Ⓑ reply
- Ⓒ *re*
- Ⓓ replay

4. Which is a synonym for *noticed*?

- Ⓐ saw
- Ⓑ wrote
- Ⓒ missed
- Ⓓ ignored

5. What is the author's purpose?

- Ⓐ to inform
- Ⓑ to persuade
- Ⓒ to define
- Ⓓ to entertain

SCORE

1. Ⓨ Ⓝ

2. Ⓨ Ⓝ

3. Ⓨ Ⓝ

4. Ⓨ Ⓝ

5. Ⓨ Ⓝ

___ / 5

Total

NAME: ______________________________ DATE: ____________________

MAKING THE TEAM

"Hurry up, Kyle," Dad called. "We need to leave for the swim-team tryouts!"

Kyle sat glumly on his bed. He liked swimming, but he was convinced he wouldn't be fast enough to impress the coach. And he definitely didn't want to embarrass himself.

"I changed my mind," he shouted back. "I've decided not to go."

Now Kyle heard the familiar *thump thump* of his father's footsteps on the staircase. Dad poked his head into Kyle's room. "Why not?" he asked. "I thought you enjoyed swimming."

"I do, but ..."

"... but you're afraid you won't make the team, right?"

Kyle glanced up. How had Dad guessed?

"Listen," Dad said. "You're probably scared, but why not at least have the coach time you? There's nothing to lose by trying, even if you don't make the team. And who knows? You might even surprise yourself."

Kyle considered that briefly. "Okay, I guess I'll go," he finally sighed.

Half an hour later, Kyle was anxiously waiting with everyone else who wanted to try out. He hated the idea of disappointing his father, so when the coach called his name, he forced himself to the edge of the swimming pool. The coach blew his whistle and Kyle plunged in, churning through the water as quickly as he could. When he reached the other side of the pool, he popped his head up and grasped the steel ladder at the pool's edge, shaking his dripping hair out of his eyes. Nervously, he climbed out of the water and returned to where the coach was standing.

"How did I do?" he practically whispered.

The coach squinted at his stopwatch and then smiled at Kyle. "You had a terrific time! In fact, you got one of the fastest times I've seen today. You'll do a fantastic job on the swim team."

NAME: ______________________ **DATE:** ______________

DIRECTIONS Read "Making the Team" and then answer the questions.

1. What is the text about?
   - Ⓐ coaching teams
   - Ⓑ trying out for band
   - Ⓒ making the swim team
   - Ⓓ playing games at school

2. What is the author's purpose?
   - Ⓐ to entertain
   - Ⓑ to persuade readers to try out for a swim team
   - Ⓒ to teach readers how to play water polo
   - Ⓓ to explain how to swim

3. How does Kyle feel after his trial swim?
   - Ⓐ proud
   - Ⓑ nervous
   - Ⓒ jealous
   - Ⓓ angry

4. Which sentence is the most climactic moment in the text?
   - Ⓐ He liked swimming, but he was convinced he wouldn't be fast enough to impress the coach.
   - Ⓑ Dad poked his head into Kyle's room.
   - Ⓒ He hated the idea of disappointing his father, so when the coach called his name, he forced himself to the edge of the swimming pool.
   - Ⓓ Kyle sat glumly on his bed.

5. Kyle's experience is most like that of someone who
   - Ⓐ wins the lottery.
   - Ⓑ forgets to study for a test and fails.
   - Ⓒ is nervous about a test but gets a good grade.
   - Ⓓ lets down a family member.

6. What is the problem?
   - Ⓐ Kyle is afraid he will hurt himself.
   - Ⓑ Kyle can't find his swimsuit.
   - Ⓒ Kyle won't listen to his father.
   - Ⓓ Kyle is afraid he won't make the team.

SCORE

1. Ⓨ Ⓝ
2. Ⓨ Ⓝ
3. Ⓨ Ⓝ
4. Ⓨ Ⓝ
5. Ⓨ Ⓝ
6. Ⓨ Ⓝ

___ / 6 Total

NAME: ______________________ **DATE:** ______________

SCORE

___ / 4

DIRECTIONS Reread "Making the Team." Then, read the prompt and respond on the lines below.

Think about a time when you tried something you didn't think you could do. Describe your experience.

NAME: ____________________ **DATE:** ____________

DIRECTIONS Read the text and then answer the questions.

Fires can be dangerous, which is why fire safety is important. Here are some things you can do to be prepared and keep your home safe:

- Always cook with an adult.
- Don't play in the kitchen.
- Keep towels and flammables (FLAM-uh-buhlz) away from the stove, fireplaces, and heaters.
- Never place clothes or flammables on a lamp.
- Don't plug too many items into an electrical outlet.
- Never play with matches or lighters.

1. What does the first sentence tell the reader about the text?

- (A) This is about the best ways to start fires.
- (B) This is about how to heat things without using fire.
- (C) This is about tragedies that occurred because of fires.
- (D) This is about how to be safe when around fires.

2. What is the main idea?

- (A) Adults should do the cooking.
- (B) Do not play with matches or lighters.
- (C) There are things you can do to be safe and prevent fires.
- (D) Fires are very dangerous.

3. The word *flammables* has

- (A) one syllable.
- (B) two syllables.
- (C) three syllables.
- (D) none of the above

4. An antonym of *always* is

- (A) never.
- (B) don't.
- (C) away.
- (D) from.

5. What is the author's purpose?

- (A) to instruct
- (B) to scare
- (C) to entertain
- (D) to persuade

SCORE

1. Ⓨ Ⓝ

2. Ⓨ Ⓝ

3. Ⓨ Ⓝ

4. Ⓨ Ⓝ

5. Ⓨ Ⓝ

___ / 5
Total

NAME: ______________________ **DATE:** ______________

DIRECTIONS Read the text and then answer the questions.

SCORE

1. Ⓨ Ⓝ

2. Ⓨ Ⓝ

3. Ⓨ Ⓝ

4. Ⓨ Ⓝ

5. Ⓨ Ⓝ

___ / 5
Total

One of the most important things your family can do to stay safe is to take good care of the smoke alarms in your home. Smoke alarms warn your family if there is a fire. Then, there is time to call the fire department and get to safety. You can help smoke alarms do their jobs. Every month, tell your parents to test the smoke alarms to be sure they are working properly. It is also important to change the batteries in your smoke alarms. The batteries should be changed every year. You can remind your parents to do that, too. Just a few minutes each month and new batteries each year can make a big difference in fire safety!

1. What does the first sentence tell the reader about the text?

- Ⓐ It is about home safety.
- Ⓑ It is about why smoke alarms should be tested.
- Ⓒ It is about how to change a smoke-alarm battery.
- Ⓓ It is about taking care of smoke alarms.

2. Which summary is **not** based on information from the text?

- Ⓐ Change the batteries in your smoke alarm every two years.
- Ⓑ Changing the batteries in smoke alarms can make a big difference.
- Ⓒ You should remind an adult to check that the smoke alarms in your home work properly.
- Ⓓ Change the batteries in your smoke alarm every year.

3. Which word part in *properly* is the suffix?

- Ⓐ *–ly*
- Ⓑ *proper*
- Ⓒ *prop–*
- Ⓓ *pro–*

4. A synonym for *properly* is

- Ⓐ important.
- Ⓑ safety.
- Ⓒ should.
- Ⓓ correctly.

5. Which word best describes the tone?

- Ⓐ frightened
- Ⓑ comical
- Ⓒ serious
- Ⓓ informal

NAME: ____________________________ **DATE:** ________________

DIRECTIONS Read the text and then answer the questions.

How do fires start? All fires need three things in order to burn: oxygen, fuel, and a heat source. Just about anything that can burn can be fuel. But some things such as wood and cloth burn more easily than others. Things that burn easily should be stored carefully so there won't be a fire. But fires also need a source of heat. Lamps, matches, lighters, and stoves are all sources of heat. Fires cannot burn unless they have oxygen, fuel, and heat. So if you keep things that burn easily away from sources of heat, you can prevent fires.

1. What is the text about?

- (A) The text is about putting out fires.
- (B) The text is about the history of fires.
- (C) The text is about how fires start.
- (D) The text is about dangerous fires.

2. Which are **not** sources of heat?

- (A) stoves
- (B) lamps
- (C) matches
- (D) oxygen

3. Which is the suffix in *easily*?

- (A) *–ly*
- (B) *easi–*
- (C) easy
- (D) *–ily*

4. What is the author's purpose?

- (A) to entertain
- (B) to persuade readers to start fires
- (C) to convince readers to become firefighters
- (D) to inform readers about fire safety

5. In which point of view is the text written?

- (A) first person
- (B) second person
- (C) third person
- (D) none of the above

SCORE

1. Ⓨ Ⓝ
2. Ⓨ Ⓝ
3. Ⓨ Ⓝ
4. Ⓨ Ⓝ
5. Ⓨ Ⓝ

___ / 5 Total

NAME: ______________________ **DATE:** ______________

THE LIFE OF A FIREFIGHTER

Would you like to be a firefighter? What do firefighters do? They put out fires. They save people. They visit schools to talk about fire safety. Firefighters do all of the above things. They do a lot of other things, too.

When a fire starts, firefighters get there fast. They work fast, too. That is because firefighters practice. It is not easy to put out fires. Firefighters have to act fast so they can put a fire out right away. They also have to work as a team. Everyone on the team has to know what to do. That takes practice. So firefighters practice together so that they will be ready for the next fire. They also learn new ways to put out fires and other new things to help them do their jobs. Then, they practice those new skills.

Firefighters help people who are hurt. When people get hurt, firefighters often get to the scene first. Firefighters know how to give first aid. Firefighters are trained to give special kinds of first aid.

Firefighters do their jobs best if they are in good shape. They also do their jobs best if their trucks and tools are clean and ready to use. So, firefighters take good care of their bodies. They also take care of their trucks and tools. They stay fit and healthy. They exercise. They also clean and fix their gear and their tools. That way, when there is a fire, all of the gear works the way it should.

The more people know about fire safety, the safer people are. Firefighters teach people about fire safety. They teach people how to prevent fires and what to do if there is a fire. Some firefighters visit schools. Other firefighters talk about fire safety on the radio and TV. Fires are dangerous and can be scary. But firefighters are there to help keep people safe.

NAME: ____________________ **DATE:** ______________

DIRECTIONS Read "The Life of a Firefighter" and then answer the questions.

1. Which alternative title does **not** fit the text?

Ⓐ A Firefighter's Job
Ⓑ What Firefighters Do
Ⓒ How to Become a Firefighter
Ⓓ Firefighters: At Work

2. A reader would most likely read the text to

Ⓐ learn more about how to put out fires.
Ⓑ be informed about fire safety.
Ⓒ be entertained by a fictional story about fire.
Ⓓ learn more about firefighters.

3. Which of the following do firefighters **not** do?

Ⓐ save people
Ⓑ put out fires
Ⓒ visit schools to talk about fire safety
Ⓓ arrest people

4. When do firefighters do their jobs best?

Ⓐ when they are in good shape
Ⓑ when they are sleepy
Ⓒ when they are loud
Ⓓ when they are dirty

5. Knowing about ______ would help the reader understand the text.

Ⓐ first aid
Ⓑ teamwork
Ⓒ health and fitness
Ⓓ all of the above

6. Which statement about firefighters is **not** true?

Ⓐ Firefighters take care of their bodies and their gear.
Ⓑ Firefighters know first aid.
Ⓒ Firefighters do not work as a team.
Ⓓ Firefighters teach people about fire safety.

SCORE

1. Ⓨ Ⓝ
2. Ⓨ Ⓝ
3. Ⓨ Ⓝ
4. Ⓨ Ⓝ
5. Ⓨ Ⓝ
6. Ⓨ Ⓝ

___ / 6 **Total**

NAME: ______________________ **DATE:** ______________

DIRECTIONS Reread "The Life of a Firefighter." Then, read the prompt and respond on the lines below.

SCORE

___ / 4

Think about what it is like to be a firefighter. Would you want to be a firefighter? Why or why not?

NAME: ______________________ **DATE:** ______________

DIRECTIONS Read the text and then answer the questions.

It was the worst day ever! First, Melissa stepped in a puddle and got muddy water on her new jeans. Then, when she got to school, she couldn't find her math homework. Melissa decided to tell her teacher what happened. She nervously went into the classroom.

"Mr. Harper, I'm sorry, but I forgot to bring my math homework today."

Mr. Harper looked up from his papers. "Did you do the homework?"

"Yes, I did. I even put it in my math folder. But I left my folder at home."

"Don't worry. The homework isn't due until tomorrow," said Mr. Harper.

What a relief! At least something went right.

1. What is this text about?

Ⓐ winning a big prize
Ⓑ a bad day
Ⓒ how to make pizza
Ⓓ planets and stars

2. Which title best fits the text?

Ⓐ A Muddy Day
Ⓑ Forgetting Homework
Ⓒ Mr. Harper's Class
Ⓓ The Worst Day Ever

3. *Nervously* is

Ⓐ a noun.
Ⓑ an adverb.
Ⓒ a verb.
Ⓓ a pronoun.

4. Which word indicates Melissa's feelings at the end of the text?

Ⓐ relief
Ⓑ least
Ⓒ tomorrow
Ⓓ worry

5. *It was the worst day ever!* is an example of

Ⓐ a metaphor.
Ⓑ hyperbole.
Ⓒ personification.
Ⓓ onomatopoeia.

SCORE

1. Ⓨ Ⓝ
2. Ⓨ Ⓝ
3. Ⓨ Ⓝ
4. Ⓨ Ⓝ
5. Ⓨ Ⓝ

___ / 5
Total

NAME: ______________________ **DATE:** ______________

DIRECTIONS Read the text and then answer the questions.

SCORE

1. Ⓨ Ⓝ

2. Ⓨ Ⓝ

3. Ⓨ Ⓝ

4. Ⓨ Ⓝ

5. Ⓨ Ⓝ

___ / 5
Total

Mr. Harper said, "I have an announcement to make." Everyone stopped working and listened closely.

"You've all worked very hard on your multiplication. You deserve a chance for a reward. I'm going to put three multiplication problems on the board. I want all of you to write the problems on a piece of paper, solve them, and hand your papers in. Then, I'll draw one paper. If I draw your paper and your answers are correct, you will win two movie passes."

"Wow!" Melissa said to Beth excitedly. "What a great prize! I love movies!"

"Me, too!" said Beth. "I hope one of us wins. Then, we can go to the movies together."

1. Which words give the reader the best preview of the text?

- Ⓐ *announcement*, *reward*, *movies*
- Ⓑ *listened*, *multiplication*, *wins*
- Ⓒ *make*, *problems*, *reward*
- Ⓓ *papers*, *closely*, *movie*

2. Which title best fits the text?

- Ⓐ Free Passes
- Ⓑ Making Announcements
- Ⓒ Multiply for Movies
- Ⓓ Going to the Movies

3. Which is the root word in *announcement*?

- Ⓐ announce
- Ⓑ ment
- Ⓒ ounce
- Ⓓ noun

4. Which word is a synonym for *prize*?

- Ⓐ correct
- Ⓑ announcement
- Ⓒ multiplication
- Ⓓ reward

5. What is the author's purpose?

- Ⓐ to entertain
- Ⓑ to inform
- Ⓒ to persuade
- Ⓓ to instruct

NAME: ______________________ **DATE:** ______________

DIRECTIONS Read the text and then answer the questions.

Mr. Harper was a good teacher. Melissa liked that he explained math so that she could understand. Today, Mr. Harper had thought of something better than ever. He wrote three multiplication problems on the board and asked everyone to solve them. Everyone who handed in a paper with the right answers had a chance to win a pair of movie passes! Not a sound could be heard as Mr. Harper pulled a paper from the stack, checked the answers on it, and looked up at the class.

"We have a winner," he said. "Melissa, you'll be going to the movies!"

Melissa excitedly jumped up. "I won!" she shouted. What a great class!

1. Which question would **not** help readers understand the text?

- (A) Who won the movie passes?
- (B) Why does Melissa like Mr. Harper's class?
- (C) How many problems did Mr. Harper write on the board?
- (D) On what day of the week did Mr. Harper have his students solve math problems?

2. What is the setting?

- (A) Melissa's house
- (B) a classroom
- (C) Mr. Harper's house
- (D) the movies

3. A homophone of *board* is

- (A) boarded
- (B) hoard
- (C) border
- (D) bored

4. Which word best describes Melissa's emotions?

- (A) good
- (B) better
- (C) great
- (D) excitedly

5. *Pulled a paper* is an example of

- (A) a simile.
- (B) alliteration.
- (C) a metaphor.
- (D) rhyming.

SCORE

1. Ⓨ Ⓝ
2. Ⓨ Ⓝ
3. Ⓨ Ⓝ
4. Ⓨ Ⓝ
5. Ⓨ Ⓝ

___ / 5
Total

NAME: ______________________ **DATE:** ______________

A MOVIE MESS

Melissa and Sandra sat in the cafeteria finishing their lunch.

"Mr. Harper asked us all to solve three multiplication problems," Melissa said. "Then, we turned our papers in. Everyone who got the right answers got into a drawing to win two movie passes. I was the winner! I'm so excited!"

"You are incredibly lucky!" Sandra said. "I love going to the movies."

"You do? If you want, we could use my passes and go to the movies this weekend."

"You're the best friend ever!" Sandra said and hugged Melissa.

Just then, Melissa's friend Beth came into the cafeteria. When Beth got to the table, she said, "Melissa, you are so unbelievably lucky! I can't wait to go to the movies with you. We should pick a movie."

Suddenly, Melissa got a sick feeling in her stomach. She had forgotten that she and Beth had promised to go to the movies together if one of them won the passes. Sandra's face fell and her eyes filled up with tears.

Melissa turned to Beth. "This is my fault. I forgot that you and I promised we would share the passes if one of us won. I asked Sandra to go to the movies instead." Then, she turned back to Sandra and said, "I'm really sorry, Sandra."

After a long silence, Beth said, "I know! Why don't we all go to the movies?"

"I can't," Sandra said softly. "I won't have enough movie money until my birthday, and that's not for three more weeks."

Then, Melissa said, "Why don't we all split the cost of a third movie ticket? That way, it will be equal for everyone."

"Really?" Sandra asked as her eyes lit up.

"It'll be fun for all three of us to go together," Beth said.

"You really are the best friend ever!" Sandra said, and hugged Melissa again.

NAME: ______________________ **DATE:** ______________

DIRECTIONS Read "A Movie Mess" and then answer the questions.

1. Which title would **not** fit the text?

Ⓐ Not Enough Tickets
Ⓑ Bad Friends
Ⓒ Problem Solving with Friends
Ⓓ Three Friends and a Movie

2. A reader would most likely read the text to

Ⓐ be entertained.
Ⓑ be persuaded to do something.
Ⓒ learn about the movies.
Ⓓ learn about multiplication.

3. How does Sandra feel when Beth says she and Melissa should pick a movie?

Ⓐ excited
Ⓑ scared
Ⓒ sad
Ⓓ curious

4. What will likely happen next?

Ⓐ Sandra will not want to go to the movies.
Ⓑ Beth will get angry at Sandra.
Ⓒ Melissa will tell Beth she does not want to go to the movies.
Ⓓ Melissa, Beth, and Sandra will go to the movies.

5. Melissa's experience relates to that of someone who

Ⓐ won amusement park tickets in a raffle.
Ⓑ accidentally invited too many friends to the zoo.
Ⓒ cannot find friends to sit with at lunch.
Ⓓ constantly borrows money from friends.

6. What lesson does Melissa learn?

Ⓐ There is usually a good solution to a problem.
Ⓑ Sandra is too sensitive.
Ⓒ It is difficult to have more than one friend.
Ⓓ Being a good friend involves lending money to your friends.

SCORE

1. Ⓨ Ⓝ
2. Ⓨ Ⓝ
3. Ⓨ Ⓝ
4. Ⓨ Ⓝ
5. Ⓨ Ⓝ
6. Ⓨ Ⓝ

___ / 6
Total

NAME: ______________________ **DATE:** ______________

DIRECTIONS Reread "A Movie Mess." Then, read the prompt and respond on the lines below.

SCORE

___ / 4

Have you ever been in a situation similar to Melissa's? How did you solve the problem?

NAME: ____________________ **DATE:** ______________

DIRECTIONS Read the text and then answer the questions.

Today, many people go to college to prepare for their careers. Others go to schools to learn the skills they will need. It wasn't always that way, though. Many years ago, people became *apprentices* (uh-PREN-tis-ez) to learn their jobs. They worked with a master who taught them their skills. Apprentices learned by watching, doing small tasks, and practicing on their own. When they were ready, they became *journeymen*. Journeymen had all the skills they needed but were not yet ready to be masters. They became masters when other masters agreed that their work was good enough.

1. What is the text about?

- (A) finding the right college
- (B) how people learned their jobs
- (C) what apprentices did
- (D) what a journeyman did

2. What is **not** a way that apprentices learned their jobs?

- (A) by doing small, easy tasks
- (B) by practicing on their own
- (C) by watching a master
- (D) by going to special schools

3. Which is a compound word?

- (A) apprentices
- (B) master
- (C) journeymen
- (D) all of the above

4. Which is a synonym for *tasks*?

- (A) chores
- (B) skills
- (C) masters
- (D) schools

5. What word best describes the tone of the text?

- (A) informational
- (B) informal
- (C) bored
- (D) lighthearted

SCORE

1. Ⓨ Ⓝ

2. Ⓨ Ⓝ

3. Ⓨ Ⓝ

4. Ⓨ Ⓝ

5. Ⓨ Ⓝ

___ / 5 **Total**

NAME:______________________________ DATE:__________________

DIRECTIONS Read the text and then answer the questions.

SCORE

1. Ⓨ Ⓝ

2. Ⓨ Ⓝ

3. Ⓨ Ⓝ

4. Ⓨ Ⓝ

5. Ⓨ Ⓝ

___ / 5 Total

What kind of job do you want when you grow up? There are many careers from which you can choose. Today, people become teachers, doctors, bus drivers, store managers, or bankers. But many years ago, people did different things. Coopers made wooden barrels for storing and shipping things. Silversmiths made candlesticks, dishes, and even jewelry. Cobblers made shoes and boots. Weavers made cloth. And tailors made clothing. Today, many of these jobs can be done by machines in factories, but there are still people who know how to do these jobs by hand.

1. Which title would best fit the text?

- Ⓐ Jobs Now and Then
- Ⓑ How to Find the Right Job
- Ⓒ The Life of a Cooper
- Ⓓ Learn to Be a Tailor

2. What did a cooper do?

- Ⓐ made shoes and boots
- Ⓑ made wooden barrels
- Ⓒ made cloth
- Ⓓ made candlesticks

3. Which word makes a new word by adding the prefix *re*–?

- Ⓐ who
- Ⓑ do
- Ⓒ many
- Ⓓ bus

4. Which is a compound word?

- Ⓐ different
- Ⓑ barrels
- Ⓒ factories
- Ⓓ candlesticks

5. *By hand* means

- Ⓐ helping someone.
- Ⓑ clapping your hands.
- Ⓒ using only one hand to do something.
- Ⓓ doing something without using a machine.

NAME: ______________________________ **DATE:** ________________

DIRECTIONS Read the text and then answer the questions.

Today, it is easy to print something. One click of a button is enough. But a long time ago, people used printing presses to print newspapers, flyers, and other papers. Printing presses are machines that transfer, or move, letters and images onto paper or cloth. Blocks with letters or pictures on them were covered with ink and then pressed onto paper. Then, the ink was allowed to dry. When it was dry, people could read what was printed. The first printing presses were worked by hand. Later, printing presses ran on steam power. Today, printing is much easier. Now we use electricity and computers to print.

1. When skimming, which words give the reader a general idea about the text?

Ⓐ *print*, *pressed*, *ink*

Ⓑ *something*, *long*, *paper*, *steam*

Ⓒ *transfer*, *button*, *printed*

Ⓓ *computers*, *electricity*, *easier*

2. Which sentence is the summary sentence of the text?

Ⓐ the last sentence

Ⓑ the second sentence

Ⓒ the first sentence

Ⓓ the third sentence

3. Which is the correct pronunciation of *machines*?

Ⓐ MACK-ines

Ⓑ mack-EENZ

Ⓒ MUH-sheenz

Ⓓ muh-SHEENZ

4. Which words are antonyms?

Ⓐ *transfer* and *move*

Ⓑ *ink* and *steam*

Ⓒ *today* and *now*

Ⓓ *easy* and *difficult*

5. What is the author's purpose?

Ⓐ to entertain

Ⓑ to instruct

Ⓒ to inform

Ⓓ to clarify

SCORE

1. Ⓨ Ⓝ

2. Ⓨ Ⓝ

3. Ⓨ Ⓝ

4. Ⓨ Ⓝ

5. Ⓨ Ⓝ

___ / 5

Total

NAME: ____________________ **DATE:** ______________

BENJAMIN FRANKLIN, PRINTER

Benjamin Franklin

Benjamin Franklin is famous for many things. He was an American leader. He was an inventor and a scientist. But did you know that he was also a printer? That was Ben's first job. Ben always loved books and reading. That is why his parents thought that being a printer would be a good job for him.

When Ben was twelve years old, he went to work. He was an apprentice. He worked with his older brother, James. James was a printer, and Ben learned the trade. He learned to use the printing press. He did other tasks around the printing shop, too. He also learned how to work with customers. He was a fast learner. James started a newspaper called *The New England Courant* (KOOR-uhnt). Ben printed the pages and got people to buy the paper. Ben did a good job as a printer. So when he was twenty-two, he was ready for his own print shop.

Ben and a friend moved from Boston to Philadelphia. Ben got a job as a journeyman printer. After a few years, he opened his own shop. He took over a newspaper called *The Pennsylvania Gazette*. It soon became very popular. Then, he printed an almanac (AWL-muh-nak). Almanacs are printed every year. They have facts about weather, tides, and other things. They also have good advice and recipes. Franklin called his almanac *Poor Richard's Almanack*. Soon, it was the most popular book in the colonies.

Ben believed that newspapers should be for everyone. He wanted people to be able to get new ideas. He wanted people to get the news. So he put cartoons and pictures in his newspaper. That way, even people who could not read could still know what was going on.

Most people think of Benjamin Franklin as a famous scientist and inventor. They also think of him as an American leader. He was all of those things. But before any of them, he was a printer.

NAME: ____________________ **DATE:** ____________

DIRECTIONS Read "Benjamin Franklin, Printer" and then answer the questions.

1. The title tells the reader that the text is about

- Ⓐ the history of printing.
- Ⓑ how to write using cursive.
- Ⓒ Benjamin Franklin's job as a printer.
- Ⓓ Benjamin Franklin's handwriting.

2. Which is the author's purpose?

- Ⓐ to entertain
- Ⓑ to inform
- Ⓒ to persuade
- Ⓓ There is no purpose.

3. How did Ben make sure that everyone could understand the news?

- Ⓐ by including cartoons and pictures
- Ⓑ by delivering newspapers
- Ⓒ by putting all the news in *Poor Richard's Almanack*
- Ⓓ by printing lots of words

4. When did Ben move to Philadelphia?

- Ⓐ after he published *The Pennsylvania Gazette*
- Ⓑ after he published *Poor Richard's Almanack*
- Ⓒ after he was an apprentice to his brother James
- Ⓓ after he opened his own printer shop

5. Which describes Benjamin Franklin?

- Ⓐ printer
- Ⓑ leader
- Ⓒ scientist
- Ⓓ all of the above

6. Which happened first?

- Ⓐ Ben moved to Philadelphia.
- Ⓑ Ben worked with his brother, James.
- Ⓒ Ben published *Poor Richard's Almanack*.
- Ⓓ Ben opened his own printer shop.

SCORE

1. Ⓨ Ⓝ
2. Ⓨ Ⓝ
3. Ⓨ Ⓝ
4. Ⓨ Ⓝ
5. Ⓨ Ⓝ
6. Ⓨ Ⓝ

___ / 6
Total

NAME: ______________________________ **DATE:** ____________________

SCORE

___ / 4

DIRECTIONS Reread "Benjamin Franklin, Printer." Then, read the prompt and respond on the lines below.

What interests you? What job would you like to have someday? Why?

NAME: ______________________________ **DATE:** ________________

DIRECTIONS Read the text and then answer the questions.

When Dylan got home from school, his mother was talking on the telephone. Dylan waved and then froze when he heard what she said next.

"Next Thursday sounds great. I can definitely be free for an interview."

An interview? Afterward, Dylan asked curiously, "What's going on?"

"I have a chance at a job doing the evening news!" said his mom.

"Really? That's great! Which TV station?" Dylan asked.

"It's not a local station. It's in Seattle," said his mom.

Dylan couldn't believe it. Seattle? They would have to move!

1. What is the problem?

Ⓐ Dylan doesn't want his mom to get a new job.

Ⓑ Dylan's mom doesn't want a new job.

Ⓒ Dylan's family might move.

Ⓓ Dylan's mom talks too loudly.

2. Where is the news station located?

Ⓐ Dylan

Ⓑ Seattle

Ⓒ Thursday

Ⓓ Local

3. Which word makes a new word by adding the suffix *–ing*?

Ⓐ next

Ⓑ would

Ⓒ interview

Ⓓ news

4. Which definition of *free* is used in the text?

Ⓐ empty

Ⓑ vacant

Ⓒ costly

Ⓓ available

5. Which definition of *froze* is used in the first paragraph?

Ⓐ stood still

Ⓑ got cold

Ⓒ tag

Ⓓ removed

SCORE

1. Ⓨ Ⓝ

2. Ⓨ Ⓝ

3. Ⓨ Ⓝ

4. Ⓨ Ⓝ

5. Ⓨ Ⓝ

___ / 5

Total

NAME: ______________________ **DATE:** ______________

DIRECTIONS Read the text and then answer the questions.

SCORE

1. Ⓨ Ⓝ
2. Ⓨ Ⓝ
3. Ⓨ Ⓝ
4. Ⓨ Ⓝ
5. Ⓨ Ⓝ

___ / 5
Total

Dylan looked through the pictures that his mother had taken during her trip to Seattle. "It looks like there are some nice places there," he said.

"It really is a great city," his mother replied. "There's the Space Needle and the Seattle Aquarium. There are plenty of things to do. It's a big metropolis."

"What's the weather like in Seattle?" Dylan asked. "I hope it's not freezing."

"The temperature usually doesn't get very cold in the winter or very hot in the summer," his mother said. "Seattle has a marine climate. It rains a lot."

"I like the rain," Dylan said.

1. Which question would help readers understand the text?

- Ⓐ Why did Dylan go to Seattle with his mother?
- Ⓑ Why is the Seattle climate always hot?
- Ⓒ Where is the Pacific Ocean?
- Ⓓ What things are there to do in Seattle?

2. What title best fits the text?

- Ⓐ America's Metropolises
- Ⓑ Seattle: A Great City
- Ⓒ Dylan's New Job
- Ⓓ The Pacific Ocean

3. The root *–polis* in the word *metropolis* probably means

- Ⓐ city.
- Ⓑ aquarium.
- Ⓒ small town.
- Ⓓ Seattle.

4. What is a synonym for *marine* as it appears in the text?

- Ⓐ military
- Ⓑ coastal
- Ⓒ inland
- Ⓓ naval

5. What is the author's purpose?

- Ⓐ to entertain
- Ⓑ to inform
- Ⓒ to persuade
- Ⓓ to instruct

NAME: ______________________ **DATE:** ______________

DIRECTIONS Read the text and then answer the questions.

Dylan and his parents spent a long time getting ready to move. They were moving to Seattle because Dylan's mother got a new job there. First, they visited Seattle to find a new place to live. Then, Dylan's parents called different moving companies. They wanted to find out how much it would cost to move. Next, they picked the right moving company. After that, they packed their things in boxes and bags. Those things would go in the moving van. They packed some clothes into suitcases to take with them. Finally, it was moving day. The movers spent the whole morning putting boxes and bags into the van. Later that day, Dylan and his family left for Seattle.

1. Which heading would help a reader preview the text?

- (A) Driving a Moving Van
- (B) Dylan's Great Adventure
- (C) Buying Suitcases
- (D) Preparing to Move

2. Which words tell the reader that the text takes place in the past?

- (A) *moving* and *putting*
- (B) *because* and *time*
- (C) *spent* and *later*
- (D) *visited* and *were*

3. Which word makes a new word by adding the prefix *re–*?

- (A) move
- (B) new
- (C) place
- (D) all of the above

4. In which point of view is the text written?

- (A) first person
- (B) second person
- (C) third person
- (D) fourth person

5. Which word expresses Dylan's emotions?

- (A) long
- (B) because
- (C) finally
- (D) none of the above

SCORE

1. Ⓨ Ⓝ

2. Ⓨ Ⓝ

3. Ⓨ Ⓝ

4. Ⓨ Ⓝ

5. Ⓨ Ⓝ

___ / 5

Total

NAME:______________________________ **DATE:**__________________

THE NOT-SO-AWFUL BUS RIDE

Dylan was positive he was going to hate his new school in Seattle. He had discovered a decent skate park nearby, which made him happy. But he didn't know anyone, so he was certain school would be horrible. On his first day, Dylan had to force himself to get on the bus. He found a seat by himself and sat staring gloomily through the window. He ignored everyone else getting on the bus. He had already convinced himself that this was going to be a terrible day.

"You mind if I sit here?" asked a boy Dylan's age.

"Whatever," Dylan said.

"What's your name?" asked the boy.

"I'm Dylan." Then, after a pause, Dylan added, "What's yours?"

"Brad. I don't recognize you. Are you new?"

"Yeah," Dylan said. "We just moved to Seattle." Dylan wasn't sure what else to say. So he asked, "Do you play sports or anything?"

"Not that much," Brad responded. "Except for skateboarding."

"You skateboard?" Dylan asked, happily surprised.

"Yeah, I love it. Do you skateboard?" asked Brad.

"Whenever I can. There's a skate park near my house," said Dylan. Then, an idea occurred to him. Almost reluctantly, he said, "Maybe we could skate sometime."

"Yeah, that'd be great," agreed Brad. "We should."

Just then, the bus pulled into the school's parking lot. Everyone got off and headed for the building. Dylan had no idea where to go. When Brad noticed Dylan hesitating, he said, "I'm going by the office if you want to come along. They can tell you what your classes are."

"Yeah, okay," Dylan said gratefully. Maybe this school wasn't going to be so bad after all.

NAME: ____________________ **DATE:** ______________

DIRECTIONS Read "The Not-So-Awful Bus Ride" and then answer the questions.

1. What would reading only the first sentence tell a reader about the text?

Ⓐ Dylan thinks he will have a bad day at his new school.
Ⓑ Dylan thinks he will have a good day at his new school.
Ⓒ Dylan thinks he will have an enjoyable bus ride.
Ⓓ Dylan thinks he will have an unpleasant bus ride.

2. A reader is most likely to read the text if he or she wants to

Ⓐ be persuaded to ride a bus.
Ⓑ be informed about public transportation.
Ⓒ be entertained by a fictional story.
Ⓓ learn how to drive a bus.

3. Why does Brad offer to show Dylan where the office is?

Ⓐ because Dylan is in trouble
Ⓑ because Dylan is sick
Ⓒ because Dylan is new and doesn't know where it is
Ⓓ because Brad is wasting time

4. How does Dylan feel about going to school on the first day?

Ⓐ unhappy
Ⓑ excited
Ⓒ embarrassed
Ⓓ guilty

5. Who would best connect with the text?

Ⓐ a bus driver
Ⓑ a new student
Ⓒ a parent
Ⓓ a teacher

6. Which book title would you expect to share a theme similar to that of the text?

Ⓐ Buddy the Bus
Ⓑ Bus Drivers of the World
Ⓒ My First Bus Buddy
Ⓓ Lonely at School

SCORE

1. Ⓨ Ⓝ
2. Ⓨ Ⓝ
3. Ⓨ Ⓝ
4. Ⓨ Ⓝ
5. Ⓨ Ⓝ
6. Ⓨ Ⓝ

___ / 6
Total

NAME: ______________________ **DATE:** ______________

SCORE

___ / 4

DIRECTIONS Reread "The Not-So-Awful Bus Ride." Then, read the prompt and respond on the lines below.

Have you ever made a new friend when you didn't expect to? What happened?

NAME: ______________________ **DATE:** ______________

DIRECTIONS Read the text and then answer the questions.

Were you thinking of visiting a beautiful city? You might want to go to Rio de Janeiro. Rio is the second largest city in Brazil. It is located on the coast. Rio has beautiful beaches. The beaches are only one factor that make Rio popular with tourists. A fun time of the year in Rio is Carnival. During this time, there are big parades. People dress in fancy costumes. There is a lot of music at Carnival. Other places in the world have Carnival, too. But Rio's Carnival is the largest in the world. Soccer is also popular in Rio. The city has four soccer teams! You could watch a game any day of the week. With its beaches, Carnival, and sports, there's always something to do in Rio.

1. Which sentence summarizes the text?

- (A) Rio is the second largest city in Brazil.
- (B) You could watch a game any day of the week.
- (C) There is a lot of music at Carnival.
- (D) With its beaches, Carnival, and sports, there's always something to do in Rio.

2. In which chapter of a book would you expect to find this information?

- (A) Chapter 1: Touring Brazil
- (B) Chapter 2: Famous Carnivals of Canada
- (C) Chapter 6: The Rio Grande
- (D) Chapter 9: Visiting Rio de Janeiro

3. What is the root word in *tourist*?

- (A) ist
- (B) our
- (C) tour
- (D) uri

4. Which is the antonym of *fancy*?

- (A) plain
- (B) dressy
- (C) elegant
- (D) purple

5. Which sentence should **not** be read literally?

- (A) the first sentence
- (B) the second sentence
- (C) the last sentence
- (D) These should all be read literally.

SCORE

1. (Y)(N)

2. (Y)(N)

3. (Y)(N)

4. (Y)(N)

5. (Y)(N)

___ / 5

Total

NAME: ______________________ **DATE:** ______________

DIRECTIONS Read the text and then answer the questions.

SCORE

1. Ⓨ Ⓝ

2. Ⓨ Ⓝ

3. Ⓨ Ⓝ

4. Ⓨ Ⓝ

5. Ⓨ Ⓝ

___ / 5 Total

The Amazon Rainforest is special. It is home to one-half of the world's species. The Amazon River flows through the rainforest. Eventually, it ends at the Atlantic Ocean. Many animals live in the river. Other animals live in the forest. The Amazon is a tropical rainforest. That means there are high temperatures and a lot of rain. The rainforest gets over fifty-nine inches of rain per year! It provides water, trees, and oxygen for us. It is home to many animals. We need to protect this special place. If we do not, we could lose it.

1. Which words could help a reader predict what this text is about?

- Ⓐ *rainforest* and *species*
- Ⓑ *Amazon* and *river*
- Ⓒ *Atlantic* and *protect*
- Ⓓ *animals* and *special*

2. Which best describes the climate of the Amazon Rainforest?

- Ⓐ dry and cold
- Ⓑ wet and cold
- Ⓒ dry and hot
- Ⓓ wet and hot

3. Which word is **not** plural?

- Ⓐ temperatures
- Ⓑ flows
- Ⓒ inches
- Ⓓ animals

4. What does the word *species* mean?

- Ⓐ stories
- Ⓑ zoos
- Ⓒ types
- Ⓓ fish

5. What is the author's purpose?

- Ⓐ to entertain
- Ⓑ to inform
- Ⓒ to scare
- Ⓓ to instruct

NAME: ____________________ **DATE:** ______________

DIRECTIONS Read the text and then answer the questions.

Goal! Everyone gets excited when a soccer team scores a goal. Soccer is one of the most popular sports in the world. In many other countries, including Brazil, soccer is not called *soccer*. It's called *football*. Whatever you call it, soccer is a thrilling game. To score a goal, a soccer team has to kick the ball into the other team's goal. Soccer teams have eleven players. Only goalies are allowed to touch the ball with their hands or arms. That is because goalies have to keep the other team from getting the ball into their own goal. The other players use their feet and sometimes their heads to move the ball.

1. What is the text mostly about?

Ⓐ how to try out for soccer
Ⓑ famous soccer players
Ⓒ the game of soccer
Ⓓ the history of soccer

2. What is soccer called in many countries?

Ⓐ kickball
Ⓑ goalball
Ⓒ football
Ⓓ thrilling

3. Which word uses a suffix that means "someone who"?

Ⓐ soccer
Ⓑ popular
Ⓒ player
Ⓓ whatever

4. Which is a synonym for *thrilling*?

Ⓐ new
Ⓑ boring
Ⓒ difficult
Ⓓ exciting

5. Which type of language is used in the text?

Ⓐ figurative
Ⓑ literal
Ⓒ fictional
Ⓓ comical

SCORE

1. Ⓨ Ⓝ
2. Ⓨ Ⓝ
3. Ⓨ Ⓝ
4. Ⓨ Ⓝ
5. Ⓨ Ⓝ

___ / 5
Total

NAME: ______________________________ **DATE:** ________________

WELCOME TO BRAZIL!

Welcome to Brazil! There are many things to see and do. The largest river in the world is here. The largest rainforest in the world is also here. There are big, exciting cities. There are also beautiful beaches. There is a lot of soccer, too.

Brazil is a very big country. It is the biggest country in South America. The Amazon River is in the north. It is the largest river in the world. It flows into the Atlantic Ocean. It adds a lot of fresh water to the ocean. The Amazon Rainforest is also in the north. It has many plants and animals. The rainforest provides oxygen, trees, and water to Earth. It is also home to more than one-half of the world's species of plants and animals. It is an important resource.

Brazil is south of the equator, so the seasons are different there. July is a summer month in the United States, but it is a winter month in Brazil. The northern part of Brazil has a tropical climate, but the southern part of Brazil has a cooler climate.

Brazil has a lot of big cities. Many of those cities are on the coast. They have beautiful beaches. There are fun things to do. Rio de Janeiro is one of those big cities. Carnival is very popular in Rio. There are big parades. There are big parties. The people dress in fancy costumes. They listen to music and dance. The capital of Brazil is Brasilia. It is also a big city. It is near the center of the country.

Do you like to play soccer? Soccer is very popular in Brazil. Many people in Brazil are good at soccer. Some of them become very famous. Many other people are soccer fans. They love to go to soccer matches. They like to watch their favorite teams on TV. If you visit Brazil, maybe you will go to a soccer match, too!

NAME: ______________________ **DATE:** ______________

DIRECTIONS Read "Welcome to Brazil!" and then answer the questions.

1. Which title does **not** provide enough information to make a prediction about the text?

Ⓐ The Amazon River
Ⓑ The Amazon Rainforest
Ⓒ Soccer—A Sport of the World
Ⓓ all of the above

2. Which sentence best describes the text's purpose?

Ⓐ The text was written to instruct.
Ⓑ The text was written to persuade.
Ⓒ The text was written to entertain.
Ⓓ The text was written to inform.

3. On which continent is Brazil?

Ⓐ Rio de Janeiro
Ⓑ North America
Ⓒ South America
Ⓓ United States

4. Which is **not** true about Carnival?

Ⓐ It is not popular.
Ⓑ There are parades.
Ⓒ People wear costumes.
Ⓓ There are big parties.

5. People who like ______ would most likely read the text.

Ⓐ cooking
Ⓑ mathematics
Ⓒ history
Ⓓ travel

6. Which is **not** true about Brazil?

Ⓐ Its capital is Brasilia.
Ⓑ It is in the Northern Hemisphere.
Ⓒ It has the largest river in the world.
Ⓓ There are many beaches.

SCORE

1. Ⓨ Ⓝ
2. Ⓨ Ⓝ
3. Ⓨ Ⓝ
4. Ⓨ Ⓝ
5. Ⓨ Ⓝ
6. Ⓨ Ⓝ

___ / 6 Total

NAME: ______________________________ **DATE:** __________________

DIRECTIONS Reread "Welcome to Brazil!" Then, read the prompt and respond on the lines below.

SCORE

___ / 4

Have you ever traveled to Brazil? What did you see and do? If you have never been there, what would you like to see and do if you go?

NAME: ______________________ **DATE:** ______________

DIRECTIONS Read the text and then answer the questions.

Carrie and her family had just eaten dinner. Carrie's mother said, "Carrie, your birthday is coming up. How would you like to celebrate?"

Carrie thought about it. "I like going to the zoo, but we went there last year. I'd rather do something different this time. Maybe we could go to a baseball game. I love baseball."

"I think that's a terrific idea!" Carrie's mother said.

"I agree," said her father. "Let's order tickets so we can get good seats."

1. Which sentence best helps the reader preview the text?

- (A) the first sentence
- (B) the second sentence
- (C) the third sentence
- (D) the last sentence

2. Where does Carrie want to go for her birthday?

- (A) the zoo
- (B) a baseball game
- (C) out to dinner
- (D) a basketball game

3. Which word makes a new word by adding the suffix *–ing*?

- (A) celebrate
- (B) zoo
- (C) idea
- (D) thought

4. Which is a compound word?

- (A) birthday
- (B) baseball
- (C) something
- (D) all of the above

5. Which contains a simile?

- (A) How would you like to celebrate?
- (B) I like going to the zoo, but we went there last year.
- (C) I love playing baseball.
- (D) none of the above

SCORE

1. Ⓨ Ⓝ
2. Ⓨ Ⓝ
3. Ⓨ Ⓝ
4. Ⓨ Ⓝ
5. Ⓨ Ⓝ

___ / 5
Total

NAME: ______________________ **DATE:** ______________

DIRECTIONS Read the text and then answer the questions.

SCORE

1. Ⓨ Ⓝ

2. Ⓨ Ⓝ

3. Ⓨ Ⓝ

4. Ⓨ Ⓝ

5. Ⓨ Ⓝ

___ / 5 Total

Carrie was getting excited. She and her family were going to a big baseball game for her birthday. Carrie's parents paid for the tickets. They would also buy snacks and drinks. But Carrie wanted a souvenir (soo-vuh-NEER) from the game to help her remember the day. She counted her money. Her grandma had sent her twenty dollars. She had also saved ten dollars on her own. That made thirty dollars. "I bet I have enough for something nice," Carrie thought. "I could buy a T-shirt or a hat."

1. What is this text about?

Ⓐ a rich grandma

Ⓑ a girl who likes T-shirts

Ⓒ a family playing baseball

Ⓓ a girl thinking about what to buy at a baseball game

2. Which part of the text does the second sentence tell about?

Ⓐ climax

Ⓑ falling action

Ⓒ conflict

Ⓓ plot

3. Which word is a compound word?

Ⓐ souvenir

Ⓑ counted

Ⓒ baseball

Ⓓ paid

4. Which two words have similar meanings?

Ⓐ *buy* and *dollars*

Ⓑ *paid* and *bought*

Ⓒ *saved* and *counted*

Ⓓ *ten* and *twenty*

5. Which sentence shows that Carrie is responsible?

Ⓐ Carrie was getting excited.

Ⓑ Carrie's parents paid for the tickets.

Ⓒ But Carrie wanted a souvenir from the game to help her remember the day.

Ⓓ She had also saved ten dollars on her own.

NAME: ______________________ **DATE:** ______________

DIRECTIONS Read the text and then answer the questions.

It was the day before Carrie's birthday. Her parents had bought tickets to a baseball game, and Carrie couldn't wait. Baseball was her favorite sport. She was even on her school's softball team. At practice, she told her coach how excited she was to go to a major-league game.

"Bring a score card so you can remember everything," the coach said.

"But I've never used a score card," Carrie said. "I don't know how."

"It's not difficult," the coach said. "I can teach you if you're interested."

"Thanks!" Carrie said. "I'd really like to learn."

The coach showed Carrie how to record stats on a score card. Soon, she understood. She was ready for the game.

1. What does Carrie learn to do?

- (A) throw a baseball
- (B) use a score card
- (C) catch a baseball
- (D) buy tickets to a game

2. What is the setting?

- (A) the bus
- (B) softball practice
- (C) Carrie's house
- (D) choir rehearsal

3. Which word makes a new word by adding the prefix *un*–?

- (A) sure
- (B) had
- (C) wait
- (D) not

4. Which is a synonym for *actual*?

- (A) sharp
- (B) fun
- (C) big
- (D) real

5. *Carrie couldn't wait* is

- (A) an onomatopoeia.
- (B) a simile.
- (C) a hyperbole.
- (D) a metaphor.

SCORE

1. Ⓨ Ⓝ
2. Ⓨ Ⓝ
3. Ⓨ Ⓝ
4. Ⓨ Ⓝ
5. Ⓨ Ⓝ

___ / 5

Total

NAME: ______________________________ **DATE:** ____________________

AN AMAZING BIRTHDAY PRESENT

Carrie and her family were on their way to the big baseball game to celebrate Carrie's birthday. The traffic was heavy, so it took them an hour to get to the stadium. After her dad parked the car, the whole family went into the stadium. They showed their tickets at the gate and then found their seats. Carrie's mom and dad had gotten good seats, so they could see everything on the field. When they sat down, Carrie thought of something.

"I forgot to get a score card! Can I go get one now?"

"I'll go with you," said Carrie's mother.

Just as Carrie and her mother returned to their seats, the game started. The two teams played well. Both teams soon scored several home runs. Carrie watched everything and kept score on her card. At the end of the fourth inning, the score was tied. "This is a good game," Carrie said. "The score's even, and both teams are playing really well."

Carrie's dad said, "Games like this are exciting because you can't be sure who's going to win."

The seventh-inning stretch came. Carrie decided that it would be a good time to choose a souvenir. Carrie and her dad went to one of the T-shirt stands to pick out a shirt for Carrie. Her mom and Scott, Carrie's little brother, went to get snacks and drinks. Everyone got back to their seats in time for the rest of the game.

When the game started again, Carrie couldn't take her eyes off the action. She kept careful score for the rest of the game. Everyone cheered loudly when the home team scored the winning run. What a great game! As Carrie and her family left the stadium, Carrie saw some of the players. Dad saw them, too, and whispered something to Mom. Then, he asked Carrie to borrow her new T-shirt. Carrie wondered what was going on, but she gave him her shirt. Then, Dad took it over to the players. Suddenly, Carrie understood what Dad was doing. He was getting the players to sign her shirt! When Dad got back with the shirt, Carrie hugged him and said, "This is the most amazing present I ever had!"

NAME: ______________________________ **DATE:** ________________

DIRECTIONS Read "An Amazing Birthday Present" and then answer the questions.

1. The title indicates that the text takes place

(A) on the Fourth of July.
(B) on someone's birthday.
(C) during the winter.
(D) on the weekend.

2. From whose perspective is the text written?

(A) Carrie's mom
(B) Carrie's
(C) Carrie's dad
(D) Scott's

3. What is Carrie's "amazing birthday present"?

(A) a score card
(B) snacks and drinks
(C) an autographed T-shirt
(D) tickets

4. Which sentence shows that Dad has a surprise for Carrie?

(A) Dad saw them, too, and whispered something to Mom.
(B) The traffic was heavy, so it took them an hour to get to the stadium.
(C) Just as Carrie and her mother returned to their seats, the game started.
(D) Dad and Carrie went to one of the T-shirt stands to pick out a shirt for Carrie.

5. Carrie's experience most closely relates to someone who

(A) loses a soccer game.
(B) watches TV shows at home.
(C) plans a party for a friend.
(D) receives a surprise gift.

6. Which book title would you expect to share a similar theme with the text?

(A) Watching the Big Game
(B) Baseball and Its History
(C) The Perfect Birthday Surprise
(D) My Big Day

SCORE

1. Ⓨ Ⓝ
2. Ⓨ Ⓝ
3. Ⓨ Ⓝ
4. Ⓨ Ⓝ
5. Ⓨ Ⓝ
6. Ⓨ Ⓝ

___ / 6
Total

NAME: ______________________________ **DATE:** ____________________

DIRECTIONS Reread "An Amazing Birthday Present." Then, read the prompt and respond on the lines below.

SCORE

___ / 4

What is the best birthday gift you have ever received or given? What would you like to receive or give for a birthday?

NAME: ______________________ **DATE:** ______________

DIRECTIONS Read the text and then answer the questions.

How many sides are there on a stop sign? You don't have to count the sides to find out. You can often tell the number of sides a figure, or shape, has just from its name. A stop sign is an octagon. The prefix *oct–* means "eight," so the word *octagon* tells you that a stop sign has eight sides. Have you ever heard of the Pentagon? It is an important building in Washington, DC. The prefix *penta–* means "five," so how many sides does the Pentagon have? If you guessed five, you're right! You know that a tricycle has three wheels. The prefix *tri–* means "three." So any shape with that prefix has three sides. What shape can you think of that begins with *tri–* and has three sides?

1. How many sides does a pentagon have?

Ⓐ four
Ⓑ six
Ⓒ five
Ⓓ three

2. What is the main idea?

Ⓐ There are eight sides on a stop sign.
Ⓑ You can often tell the number of sides a shape has just from its name.
Ⓒ The Pentagon is an important building.
Ⓓ Shapes have sides.

3. Which prefix is defined in the text?

Ⓐ *penta–*
Ⓑ *tri–*
Ⓒ *oct–*
Ⓓ all of the above

4. Which is a synonym for *shape*?

Ⓐ figure
Ⓑ octagon
Ⓒ tricycle
Ⓓ sides

5. Which best describes the tone?

Ⓐ absurd
Ⓑ silly
Ⓒ depressing
Ⓓ engaging

SCORE

1. Ⓨ Ⓝ
2. Ⓨ Ⓝ
3. Ⓨ Ⓝ
4. Ⓨ Ⓝ
5. Ⓨ Ⓝ

___ / 5 Total

NAME: ______________________________ **DATE:** ________________

DIRECTIONS Read the text and then answer the questions.

SCORE

1. Ⓨ Ⓝ

2. Ⓨ Ⓝ

3. Ⓨ Ⓝ

4. Ⓨ Ⓝ

5. Ⓨ Ⓝ

___ / 5

Total

The parts of a word can tell you a lot about what that word means. You can often guess what new words mean by looking at their parts. For example, an octagon has eight sides. You can tell because *octagon* begins with the prefix *oct–*, which means "eight." But did you know that an octagon also has eight angles? Just look at the suffix *–gon*. That suffix means "angle." So the word *octagon* tells you that a figure has eight angles. Now think about the word *decagon*. If you know that *deca–* means "ten," and *–gon* means "angle," you can guess that a decagon has ten sides and ten angles. Decagons and octagons are both polygons. *Poly–* means more than one. So a polygon is a closed figure with more than one angle.

1. Which title best fits the text?

- Ⓐ It's All in the Word
- Ⓑ Octagons We See Every Day
- Ⓒ How to Draw a Shape
- Ⓓ What Does *Deca–* Mean?

2. Which index entry would help a reader locate this information?

- Ⓐ eight
- Ⓑ angles
- Ⓒ prefixes and suffixes
- Ⓓ octagons

3. Which word uses the same suffix as *decagon*?

- Ⓐ dragon
- Ⓑ polygon
- Ⓒ along
- Ⓓ song

4. Which word is defined in the text?

- Ⓐ figure
- Ⓑ octagon
- Ⓒ sides
- Ⓓ parts

5. What is the author's purpose?

- Ⓐ to entertain
- Ⓑ to persuade
- Ⓒ to inform
- Ⓓ to instruct

NAME: ______________________ **DATE:** ______________

DIRECTIONS Read the text and then answer the questions.

You may not realize it, but when you're learning math, you're also learning Greek. The ancient Greeks studied mathematics, and their language had all sorts of math-related words. For example, you know that a triangle is a three-sided figure with three angles. The prefix *tri–* comes from the Greek word for *three*. A six-sided figure with six angles is called a *hexagon*. That word comes from *hexa*, the Greek word for *six*, and *gon*, which means *angle*. The word *tetrad* means a group of four. That word comes from the Greek word for *four*, which is *tetra*. Learning Greek helps you learn math, and learning math helps you learn Greek!

1. Which is the Greek word for *four*?

- (A) gon
- (B) tri
- (C) hexa
- (D) tetra

2. Which is the topic sentence?

- (A) The ancient Greeks studied mathematics, and their language had all sorts of math-related words.
- (B) A six-sided figure with six angles is called a *hexagon*.
- (C) Learning Greek helps you learn math, and learning math helps you learn Greek!
- (D) The word *tetrad* means a group of four.

3. In the word *hexagon*, *–gon* is a

- (A) suffix.
- (B) prefix.
- (C) verb.
- (D) noun.

4. The words *hexagon* and *tetragon* share the same

- (A) prefix.
- (B) suffix.
- (C) root word.
- (D) meaning.

5. What is the author's tone?

- (A) informal and informative
- (B) formal and condescending
- (C) comical and silly
- (D) persuasive and opinionated

SCORE

1. Ⓨ Ⓝ

2. Ⓨ Ⓝ

3. Ⓨ Ⓝ

4. Ⓨ Ⓝ

5. Ⓨ Ⓝ

___ / 5

Total

NAME: ______________________ DATE: ______________

POLYGONS ARE EVERYWHERE!

You already know a lot about shapes. You learn about shapes in your math class. Maybe you have learned about polygons. *Polygons* are closed shapes. They have more than one side. They have more than one angle. But polygons aren't just in your math class. They are in many places. Look around you. You can see polygons all over.

What shape is a slice of pizza? Most slices of pizza are triangles. Triangles are polygons. What makes them polygons? They have three sides and three angles.

A pentagon is a polygon. It has five sides and five angles. There is a very big pentagon in Washington, DC. This pentagon is a building. It has five sides and five angles, so it is called the *Pentagon*. The Pentagon is a very important place. Our army and navy leaders work in the Pentagon. They help to keep our country safe. If you visit Washington, DC, maybe you can go to the Pentagon. If you do, you will be inside a polygon!

Hexagons are also polygons. Hexagons have six sides and six angles. Where can you find a hexagon? Just look for bees! When bees make honey, they store it in honeycombs. Each cell of a honeycomb is a hexagon. If you see a honeycomb, you will see a hexagon. You will also see a polygon. But be careful of the bees!

How many sides does an octagon have? An octagon has eight sides. It also has eight angles. You can tell because the word starts with *oct–*. That prefix means *eight*. Octagons have more than one side. They have more than one angle. So they are polygons. You see octagons all the time. Can you guess where? Every time you see a stop sign! Stop signs have eight sides and eight angles. That makes them octagons.

NAME: ______________________ **DATE:** ______________

DIRECTIONS Read "Polygons Are Everywhere!" and then answer the questions.

1. Which title does **not** provide enough information to make a prediction about the text?

Ⓐ Polygons All Around Me
Ⓑ My Favorite Pizza
Ⓒ Polygons and Prefixes
Ⓓ Polygons and Their Meaning

2. A reader would most likely read the text to be

Ⓐ persuaded to do something.
Ⓑ entertained by a fictional story.
Ⓒ instructed how to make a pizza.
Ⓓ informed about everyday shapes and prefixes.

3. Which polygon is **not** defined in the text?

Ⓐ octagon
Ⓑ hexagon
Ⓒ pentagon
Ⓓ nonagon

4. Which is **not** true about polygons?

Ⓐ They are closed shapes.
Ⓑ They have more than one side.
Ⓒ They are hard to find.
Ⓓ They have more than one angle.

5. People who like ______ will probably like this text.

Ⓐ music
Ⓑ art
Ⓒ mathematics
Ⓓ sports

6. Which statement is true?

Ⓐ A triangle is not a polygon.
Ⓑ Honeycombs are octagons.
Ⓒ You can see polygons in many places.
Ⓓ The Pentagon has six sides and six angles.

SCORE

1. Ⓨ Ⓝ
2. Ⓨ Ⓝ
3. Ⓨ Ⓝ
4. Ⓨ Ⓝ
5. Ⓨ Ⓝ
6. Ⓨ Ⓝ

___ / 6
Total

NAME: ______________________ **DATE:** ______________

DIRECTIONS Reread "Polygons Are Everywhere!" Then, read the prompt and respond on the line below.

SCORE

___ / 4

Which polygons appear most in your everyday life? How do you use these polygons?

NAME: ______________________ **DATE:** ______________

DIRECTIONS Read the text and then answer the questions.

One morning, Travis came downstairs for breakfast. On the table were some tickets. When Mom came into the kitchen, Travis asked her about them.

"Those are airline tickets," Mom said. "Our family is taking a vacation."

"Seriously? Where are we going?" asked Travis. He was getting excited.

"We're going to visit Aunt Sondra and Uncle Pete," Mom answered happily.

"That's totally awesome!" Travis shouted. Aunt Sondra and Uncle Pete were his favorite relatives. He hadn't seen them in months, and he missed them. He missed his cousin, Jason, too. Now he could start to plan all kinds of things he and Jason could do together.

1. How does Travis feel when Mom tells him about the vacation?

- Ⓐ afraid
- Ⓑ jealous
- Ⓒ upset
- Ⓓ happy

2. What is the setting?

- Ⓐ a kitchen
- Ⓑ Aunt Sondra's house
- Ⓒ Travis's bedroom
- Ⓓ Jason's bedroom

3. Which words share the same suffix?

- Ⓐ *together* and *her*
- Ⓑ *shouted* and *excited*
- Ⓒ *answered* and *awesome*
- Ⓓ *missed* and *months*

4. Which word is a synonym for *answered*?

- Ⓐ asked
- Ⓑ replied
- Ⓒ shouted
- Ⓓ wondered

5. The word *airline* tells that Travis and his family will travel by

- Ⓐ bus.
- Ⓑ train.
- Ⓒ car.
- Ⓓ airplane.

SCORE

1. Ⓨ Ⓝ
2. Ⓨ Ⓝ
3. Ⓨ Ⓝ
4. Ⓨ Ⓝ
5. Ⓨ Ⓝ

___ / 5 Total

NAME: ______________________ **DATE:** ______________

DIRECTIONS Read the text and then answer the questions.

SCORE

1. Ⓨ Ⓝ
2. Ⓨ Ⓝ
3. Ⓨ Ⓝ
4. Ⓨ Ⓝ
5. Ⓨ Ⓝ

___ / 5 Total

Travis needed a new suitcase. He and his family were planning a vacation, and Travis only had a backpack. His backpack was too small for everything he wanted to pack. So Dad took Travis shopping for a suitcase.

"I'd like a duffel bag," Travis said. "Duffel bags have straps. I can put the strap across my shoulder. Then, I can carry the duffel bag on my back."

"Excellent idea," Dad said. "We'll see if they have a good one."

In just a few minutes, Dad and Travis found exactly the kind Travis wanted—a green duffel bag with a black strap. Now Travis could start packing!

1. Why does Travis want a duffel bag?

Ⓐ His best friend has a duffel bag.
Ⓑ He wants a backpack.
Ⓒ He wants a bag with a strap.
Ⓓ Dad says that duffel bags do not cost much money.

2. What is Travis's problem?

Ⓐ His backpack is too small.
Ⓑ He does not want to go on vacation.
Ⓒ He is angry with Dad.
Ⓓ Duffel bags are too expensive.

3. Which word has three syllables?

Ⓐ suitcase
Ⓑ backpack
Ⓒ planning
Ⓓ excellent

4. Which is a compound word?

Ⓐ suitcase
Ⓑ everything
Ⓒ backpack
Ⓓ all of the above

5. Which phrase tells the reader that Dad agrees with Travis?

Ⓐ *...could start packing!*
Ⓑ *excellent idea*
Ⓒ *His backpack was too small.*
Ⓓ *Duffel bags have straps.*

NAME: ______________________ **DATE:** ________________

DIRECTIONS Read the text and then answer the questions.

Hi Travis,

I can't believe you'll be here in only eight days! Mom says you'll be staying for a week. I've thought of a million things we can do while you're here. Dad says you'll be flying on an airplane. You're so lucky! I want to know everything that happens on your flight, so don't forget anything, okay? I heard that pilots sometimes let kids go up into the flight deck of the plane where the pilots sit. Kids get to see the instruments that the pilots use to fly the plane. Maybe you will get to have your picture taken with the pilots!

See you before you know it.

Jason

1. Jason wants Travis to

- (A) think of things to do.
- (B) remember everything that happens on the flight.
- (C) stay away from the cockpit.
- (D) go on a business trip.

2. Which title best fits the text?

- (A) Eight Days until Summer
- (B) Playing Instruments
- (C) Business Trips
- (D) Visiting Cousins

3. Which shows the correct pronunciation of *instruments*?

- (A) in-STRUH-muhnts
- (B) in-struh-MUHNTS
- (C) IN-struh-muhnts
- (D) none of the above

4. Which is an antonym of *lucky*?

- (A) fortunate
- (B) unfortunate
- (C) privileged
- (D) happy

5. *I've thought of a million things we can do while you're here* is an example of

- (A) alliteration.
- (B) hyperbole.
- (C) simile.
- (D) metaphor.

SCORE

1. Ⓨ Ⓝ

2. Ⓨ Ⓝ

3. Ⓨ Ⓝ

4. Ⓨ Ⓝ

5. Ⓨ Ⓝ

___ / 5 Total

NAME: ______________________ **DATE:** ______________

A SMOOTH RIDE

Travis and his family were going on vacation. They would be visiting Travis's Aunt Sondra, Uncle Pete, and his cousin Jason for a week. His dad loaded all the suitcases in the car. Then, it was time to leave.

"Dad," Travis asked anxiously, "did you remember to put my duffel bag in the car? I didn't see you load it."

"Don't worry, Travis," his dad told him. "Everything's packed, including your duffel bag."

When the family got to the airport, they unloaded their suitcases. Next, they found the right place to check in for their flight. Then, it was time to get boarding passes. The passes would let them get on the plane. Once everyone had boarding passes, the next step was to go through the security line so everyone would have a safe flight. Finally, Travis and his family got to their gate—the waiting area for their plane.

The plane arrived on time. When the pilot and crew were ready for them, everyone boarded and Travis and his family found their seats. Travis gazed at everything. He wanted to remember every detail so he could describe it to Jason. When the flight was ready to take off, Travis and his family buckled their seat belts. Then, they watched a safety video.

Suddenly, Travis felt the plane jerk and then start to move. "We're taking off!" he said.

"That's right," his mom said. "Soon we'll be in the air."

Later, Travis was looking out the window when his mom nudged him. He turned around. A crew member was standing there. She said, "Would you like to see the flight deck after we land?"

"I'd love to!" Travis said. After they landed, Travis went up to the flight deck and met the pilots while the other passengers got off the plane. He even got his picture taken in the pilot's seat. "Wow!" he thought. "Wait until I tell Jason about this!"

NAME: ______________________________ **DATE:** ________________

DIRECTIONS Read "A Smooth Ride" and then answer the questions.

1. The title tells the reader that the text is about

Ⓐ a family pet with soft fur.
Ⓑ riding on a bumpy roller coaster.
Ⓒ riding bikes on a trail.
Ⓓ a pleasant airplane ride.

2. From which point of view is the text written?

Ⓐ third person
Ⓑ first person
Ⓒ second person
Ⓓ multiple points of view

3. Whom is Travis going to visit?

Ⓐ his mom
Ⓑ his uncle, aunt, and cousin
Ⓒ his dad
Ⓓ his brother

4. Which happens first?

Ⓐ Everyone goes through the security line.
Ⓑ The family finds the right place to check in for their flight.
Ⓒ The family boards the plane.
Ⓓ Everyone gets boarding passes.

5. Travis's experience most closely relates to someone who

Ⓐ rides a bike for the first time.
Ⓑ travels on a train for the first time to visit a relative.
Ⓒ travels on an airplane frequently.
Ⓓ always travels by car to visit relatives.

6. Why is Travis anxious at the beginning of the story?

Ⓐ He is afraid Dad forgot to pack his duffel bag.
Ⓑ He does not want to go on vacation.
Ⓒ He is afraid to go on an airplane.
Ⓓ He forgot all of his money.

SCORE

1. Ⓨ Ⓝ
2. Ⓨ Ⓝ
3. Ⓨ Ⓝ
4. Ⓨ Ⓝ
5. Ⓨ Ⓝ
6. Ⓨ Ⓝ

___ / 6
Total

NAME: ______________________ **DATE:** ______________

DIRECTIONS Reread "A Smooth Ride." Then, read the prompt and respond on the lines below.

SCORE

___ / 4

Have you ever been on a plane ride? If not, what do you think it would be like to fly on a plane? Write about your experience flying, or what you think it would be like.

NAME: ______________________________ **DATE:** ________________

DIRECTIONS Read the text and then answer the questions.

Try this experiment. Hold a pencil in your hand and then let go of it. What happens when you let go? The pencil falls to the ground. Why does that happen? It happens because *gravity* is at work. Gravity is a force that pulls objects toward each other. When you drop a pencil, gravity pulls the pencil toward Earth. Everything has gravity. So why doesn't the floor move toward the pencil? Larger and heavier objects have more gravity than smaller and lighter objects do. Earth is much larger and heavier than the pencil is. So Earth's pull is stronger than the pencil's pull. The sun is much larger and heavier than Earth is. That means the sun's gravity is much stronger. That's the reason that Earth orbits the sun. The sun's gravity is pulling Earth toward it.

1. Would reading the first sentence help the reader preview the text?

- (A) Yes. It introduces the topic.
- (B) Yes. It describes what will happen.
- (C) Yes. It provides a good deal of information.
- (D) No. The topic sentence comes later in the text.

2. Which index entry would help a reader find this information?

- (A) experiments
- (B) gravity
- (C) sun, the
- (D) Earth, the

3. Which is syllable is stressed in the word *gravity*?

- (A) the first syllable
- (B) the second syllable
- (C) the third syllable
- (D) none of the above

4. A synonym for *experiment* is

- (A) game.
- (B) test.
- (C) outfit.
- (D) book.

5. What is the author's purpose?

- (A) to persuade
- (B) to entertain
- (C) to confuse
- (D) to inform

SCORE

1. (Y)(N)
2. (Y)(N)
3. (Y)(N)
4. (Y)(N)
5. (Y)(N)

___ / 5

Total

NAME: ______________________ **DATE:** ______________

DIRECTIONS Read the text and then answer the questions.

SCORE

1. Ⓨ Ⓝ

2. Ⓨ Ⓝ

3. Ⓨ Ⓝ

4. Ⓨ Ⓝ

5. Ⓨ Ⓝ

___ / 5 Total

When your hands are cold, what is the solution to the problem? Maybe you rub your hands together. Your hands get warm when you rub them against each other. Why does that happen? It's because of friction. *Friction* is a force that happens whenever any two objects move against each other. Friction is needed to push the objects past each other. Friction creates energy. When you rub your hands together, that energy creates the heat you feel. Rough objects, such as sidewalks, have more friction than smooth objects, such as ice. That is why it is easier to walk on a sidewalk than it is to skate on ice. We need friction. Friction helps you walk and makes the brakes on your bike work. It is an important force.

1. Which question would help readers understand the text?

Ⓐ What causes friction?
Ⓑ Why are my hands cold?
Ⓒ Why does friction make moving easier?
Ⓓ Why is friction unimportant?

2. Which index entry would help a reader find this text's information?

Ⓐ hands
Ⓑ energy
Ⓒ brakes
Ⓓ friction

3. Which word has the same root word as *creates*?

Ⓐ eater
Ⓑ crust
Ⓒ ate
Ⓓ creation

4. Which words are antonyms?

Ⓐ *cold* and *warm*
Ⓑ *rough* and *smooth*
Ⓒ *solution* and *problem*
Ⓓ all of the above

5. Which other type of text would have a similar tone?

Ⓐ a construction magazine
Ⓑ a science book
Ⓒ an instruction manual for riding bikes
Ⓓ a history textbook

NAME: ______________________ **DATE:** ______________

DIRECTIONS Read the text and then answer the questions.

If you kick a soccer ball, it will move. But if you do not kick it, it stays where it is. Why doesn't the soccer ball move? *Inertia* (in-UR-shuh) keeps it in place. Inertia is a kind of rule about objects. Inertia tells us two things:

- Objects that are not moving will remain unmoved unless something moves them.
- Objects that are moving will keep moving unless something stops them.

Try it! Put a book on your desk and watch it. The book doesn't move because inertia is keeping it in place. Now pick up the book and drop it on the floor. The book will keep falling until the floor stops it. That's because of inertia, too!

1. What is the text about?

Ⓐ playing soccer
Ⓑ inertia
Ⓒ refusing to move
Ⓓ books about autumn

2. Which title best describes the main idea?

Ⓐ Following the Rules
Ⓑ The Rules of Inertia
Ⓒ Falling Books
Ⓓ Watching Objects Move

3. How many syllables does *inertia* have?

Ⓐ one syllable
Ⓑ two syllables
Ⓒ three syllables
Ⓓ four syllables

4. Which is an antonym of *moves*?

Ⓐ propels
Ⓑ travels
Ⓒ remains
Ⓓ moving

5. How do you know the author's purpose is to inform?

Ⓐ The language is academic and informative.
Ⓑ The language is informal and comical.
Ⓒ The language is persuasive and opinionated.
Ⓓ The language is casual and conversational.

SCORE

1. Ⓨ Ⓝ
2. Ⓨ Ⓝ
3. Ⓨ Ⓝ
4. Ⓨ Ⓝ
5. Ⓨ Ⓝ

___ / 5
Total

NAME: ______________________ **DATE:** ______________

GET MOVING!

You move every day. Every time you sit down, walk, ride a bike, or eat food, you are moving. You even move while you are sitting in a chair. What gets you moving, keeps you moving, and helps you to move the way you want to move?

One force that helps you move is gravity. Gravity pulls objects toward each other, and so gravity pulls you toward Earth. Why? Earth is bigger and heavier than you are, so you're pulled by Earth's gravity. How does that help you? When you take a step, gravity pulls on your foot. That pulling helps you put your foot down. Then, you can move your other foot. When you sit down, gravity keeps you stationary in your seat. Do you like to play baseball? Gravity makes the baseball fall after it is hit. Then, as gravity pulls the ball toward the ground, you can catch the ball.

Friction also helps you move. Friction happens when two objects rub against each other. How does friction help you move? When you walk, friction keeps your feet from slipping. When you hold a pencil, friction helps keep it in your hand. When you eat, friction helps you to chew your food, and friction makes the brakes on your bike work, too.

Inertia also helps you. Inertia is a sort of rule; it tells us two things: Things that are in motion will remain in motion until something stops them; and things that are at rest will stay at rest unless something moves them. How do these two things help you? When you ride your bike, it will keep going until you stop it, and when you sit down to read, you will stay where you are until you are ready to move.

The next time you move, think about gravity. Think about friction. Think about inertia. All of them help to get you where you want to go.

NAME:______________________ DATE:______________

DIRECTIONS Read "Get Moving!" and then answer the questions.

1. The title and photograph tell the reader that this text will be about

- (A) moving out of town.
- (B) moving your body.
- (C) how to best move boxes.
- (D) why moving is a bad idea.

2. A reader would most likely read this to

- (A) be entertained by a fictional story.
- (B) be persuaded to do something.
- (C) be informed about a new topic.
- (D) pass the time.

3. When you take a step, what pulls your foot toward Earth?

- (A) friction
- (B) gravity
- (C) a bike
- (D) sitting

4. What is the topic sentence of the second paragraph?

- (A) Then, as gravity pulls the ball toward the ground, you can catch the ball.
- (B) One force that helps you move is gravity.
- (C) Do you like to play baseball?
- (D) Earth is bigger and heavier than you are, so you are pulled by Earth's gravity.

5. People who like ______ will probably like this text.

- (A) science
- (B) technology
- (C) mathematics
- (D) sports

6. Which concept is **not** discussed in this text?

- (A) gravity
- (B) inertia
- (C) tension
- (D) friction

SCORE

1. Ⓨ Ⓝ

2. Ⓨ Ⓝ

3. Ⓨ Ⓝ

4. Ⓨ Ⓝ

5. Ⓨ Ⓝ

6. Ⓨ Ⓝ

___ / 6
Total

NAME: ______________________ **DATE:** ______________

DIRECTIONS Reread "Get Moving!" Then, read the prompt and respond on the lines below.

SCORE

___ / 4

Imagine that gravity does not exist. What do you think it would it be like to walk without gravity?

NAME: ______________________________ **DATE:** ________________

DIRECTIONS Read the text and then answer the questions.

Donna saw a notice on the bulletin board as she was leaving school. The notice announced a meeting to join the new school band. Donna carefully wrote down the information. Then, she excitedly ran off to catch the bus. At dinner, Donna told her parents about the band. "Can I join?" she pleaded. "There's an informational meeting next Wednesday. Could we go?"

Donna's mom said, "Learning music takes time and practice. Are you willing to do that?"

"I know I'll have to practice a lot," Donna said. "Please, can I join?"

Her dad said, "Let's go to the meeting. Then we'll decide."

"That sounds reasonable," Mom agreed. Donna grinned happily.

1. What does Donna want to do?

- (A) post a notice
- (B) catch the bus
- (C) announce a meeting
- (D) join the school band

2. Which title best fits the text?

- (A) Joining the School Band
- (B) Fund-raising for the Arts
- (C) Practice Makes Perfect
- (D) Bulletin Board Notices

3. Which is the root word in *information*?

- (A) form
- (B) inform
- (C) in
- (D) mate

4. Which word indicates Donna's emotions?

- (A) pleaded
- (B) excitedly
- (C) grinned
- (D) all of the above

5. Which phrase indicates that Donna is in a hurry?

- (A) saw a notice on the bulletin board
- (B) excitedly ran off
- (C) carefully wrote down the information
- (D) takes time and practice

SCORE

1. Ⓨ Ⓝ

2. Ⓨ Ⓝ

3. Ⓨ Ⓝ

4. Ⓨ Ⓝ

5. Ⓨ Ⓝ

___ / 5
Total

NAME: ______________________ **DATE:** ______________

DIRECTIONS Read the text and then answer the questions.

SCORE

1. Ⓨ Ⓝ

2. Ⓨ Ⓝ

3. Ⓨ Ⓝ

4. Ⓨ Ⓝ

5. Ⓨ Ⓝ

___ / 5
Total

Donna and her parents went to Donna's school. They were there for a meeting. The school was forming a band. Many people were there.

Mrs. Taylor, the band director, said, "Thanks for coming. We're very excited about our new band! I'm happy that all of you are interested. If you want to join the band, you must first choose your instrument. Come to the music room after school on Monday, and I will help you do that. Then, you need to rent or buy your instrument. Next, you must attend band practice every Monday, Wednesday, and Thursday. You'll also have to practice every day at home."

1. What is the second step to joining the band?

- Ⓐ to rent or buy your instrument
- Ⓑ to choose your instrument
- Ⓒ to practice every day at home
- Ⓓ to come to band practice

2. Who is the band director?

- Ⓐ Donna
- Ⓑ Donna's parents
- Ⓒ Mrs. Taylor
- Ⓓ There is no band director

3. What does the suffix *–or* mean in the word *director*?

- Ⓐ the most
- Ⓑ a person who
- Ⓒ the least
- Ⓓ the study of

4. Which is a synonym for *choose*?

- Ⓐ buy
- Ⓑ select
- Ⓒ rent
- Ⓓ practice

5. Which best describes the dialogue?

- Ⓐ informative
- Ⓑ conversational
- Ⓒ comical
- Ⓓ serious

NAME: ____________________ **DATE:** ____________

DIRECTIONS Read the text and then answer the questions.

When school was over on Monday, Donna flew to the music room. She wanted to choose an instrument so she could play in the band. When she arrived, she said, "Hi, Mrs. Taylor. I'm here to choose an instrument."

"I'm so glad you're interested in the band, Donna," said Mrs. Taylor. "Is there any instrument that particularly interests you? The flute? The violin?"

"I heard that the clarinet is easy, and I like the way it sounds," Donna answered. "That's the instrument I'd like."

"Well, the clarinet isn't especially difficult, but it takes daily practice to learn it well," said Mrs. Taylor. "You will have to practice. Our first band practice will be one week from today."

1. Which sentence gives an accurate preview of the text?
   - Ⓐ the first sentence
   - Ⓑ the second sentence
   - Ⓒ the third sentence
   - Ⓓ the fourth sentence

2. What is the setting?
   - Ⓐ the playground
   - Ⓑ the music room
   - Ⓒ the cafeteria
   - Ⓓ Donna's house

3. Which share the same suffix?
   - Ⓐ *interested* and *answered*
   - Ⓑ *wanted* and *instrument*
   - Ⓒ *answered* and *especially*
   - Ⓓ *instrument* and *trumpet*

4. A synonym for *difficult* is
   - Ⓐ easy.
   - Ⓑ simple.
   - Ⓒ uncomplicated.
   - Ⓓ challenging.

5. *Donna flew to the music room* is an example of
   - Ⓐ literal language.
   - Ⓑ figurative language.
   - Ⓒ formal language.
   - Ⓓ misleading language.

SCORE

1. Ⓨ Ⓝ

2. Ⓨ Ⓝ

3. Ⓨ Ⓝ

4. Ⓨ Ⓝ

5. Ⓨ Ⓝ

___ / 5
Total

NAME: ______________________________ **DATE:** ________________

MAKING MUSIC

It was Donna's first day of band practice. Her dad and mom had gotten her a clarinet and a music book. They got her a music stand, too. Donna had tried and tried to play the clarinet, but her music didn't sound very good. Her dad reassured her, though. He said that nobody sounds very good when they first start to play an instrument. Mom said that if Donna practiced every day, she would learn to play well.

Donna hurried to the music room as soon as school was over. She wasn't the only one. There were about twenty other kids there, each with an instrument. There were even two other people with clarinets. Mrs. Taylor, the band director, asked everyone to have a seat. When all of the students were seated, Mrs. Taylor passed around music books. Everyone got one. Then, she asked if anyone had tried to play their instruments. Donna and a few other students raised their hands.

"I'm glad you've started to practice because daily practice is very important," said Mrs. Taylor. "But so is having fun. So don't practice for too long at a time. Now, let's get started."

Mrs. Taylor taught everyone the notes they would need to know. She also taught them some songs and asked them to practice those songs at home. Then, she asked if anyone had any questions.

"I have a question," Donna said. "I tried to play the clarinet earlier this week, and the music didn't sound good at all. What am I doing wrong?"

"Probably nothing," Mrs. Taylor answered. "It takes everybody a while to play well. Practice your notes and these songs every day. I'll bet you'll sound better in no time."

Donna wasn't sure she could ever sound good. But she decided to at least try. To her surprise, after a few weeks, she was playing better. Soon, she could play songs she never thought she could play. "I really like the clarinet," Donna decided. "Maybe I'll even be a musician."

NAME: ______________________ **DATE:** ______________

DIRECTIONS Read "Making Music" and then answer the questions.

1. Which alternate title would fit this text?

- (A) Joining the School Band
- (B) Choosing an Instrument
- (C) Flying to Music
- (D) Band Practice

2. A purpose for reading this is to

- (A) be entertained.
- (B) be persuaded to do something.
- (C) be informed about a new topic.
- (D) pass the time.

3. Which word describes Mrs. Taylor?

- (A) mean
- (B) happy
- (C) encouraging
- (D) rude

4. Mom and Dad probably think it is a ______ idea for Donna to learn the clarinet.

- (A) dangerous
- (B) good
- (C) terrible
- (D) scary

5. Which saying best fits the text?

- (A) All that glitters is not gold.
- (B) Actions speak louder than words.
- (C) A penny saved is a penny earned.
- (D) Practice makes perfect.

6. What is Donna worried about?

- (A) She thinks she will never be able to play well.
- (B) She cannot find her clarinet.
- (C) She thinks Mrs. Taylor doesn't like her.
- (D) She thinks her parents are angry with her.

SCORE

1. (Y)(N)
2. (Y)(N)
3. (Y)(N)
4. (Y)(N)
5. (Y)(N)
6. (Y)(N)

___ / 6
Total

NAME: ______________________ **DATE:** ______________

DIRECTIONS Reread "Making Music." Then, read the prompt and respond on the lines below.

SCORE

___ / 4

Do you play a musical instrument? What instrument do you play? If you do not play a musical instrument, what instrument would you like to play?

NAME: ______________________ **DATE:** ______________

DIRECTIONS Read the text and then answer the questions.

What do you enjoy eating for lunch? If you said "a sandwich," you're not alone. Millions of people eat sandwiches every day. The sandwich has been popular since ancient times, but it got its name in 1762. John Montagu was a nobleman. He was not a king or a prince, but he was a ruler and a leader. His title was the Earl of Sandwich—yes, Sandwich is a real place in England! One night, he was playing a card game. He was so interested in his game that he didn't want to stop playing cards even though he was hungry. So he ordered food he could eat while he was playing. He asked for some slices of beef to be placed between two pieces of bread. Today, we use the word *sandwich* to describe his meal.

1. What is the main idea?

Ⓐ the life of John Montagu
Ⓑ how the sandwich got its name
Ⓒ ancient history
Ⓓ roast beef

2. Which sentence is **not** true?

Ⓐ The sandwich is a new invention.
Ⓑ The sandwich is very popular.
Ⓒ The sandwich got its name from John Montagu, Earl of Sandwich.
Ⓓ Millions of people eat sandwiches.

3. Which syllable is stressed in the word *nobleman*?

Ⓐ the first syllable
Ⓑ the second syllable
Ⓒ the third syllable
Ⓓ none of the above

4. Which definition of *ruler* is used in the text?

Ⓐ a child
Ⓑ a straight stick
Ⓒ a measuring tool
Ⓓ a person in charge

5. Which best describes the tone?

Ⓐ engaging
Ⓑ informal
Ⓒ gloomy
Ⓓ silly

SCORE

1. Ⓨ Ⓝ
2. Ⓨ Ⓝ
3. Ⓨ Ⓝ
4. Ⓨ Ⓝ
5. Ⓨ Ⓝ

___ / 5
Total

NAME: ____________________ **DATE:** ____________

DIRECTIONS Read the text and then answer the questions.

SCORE

1. Ⓨ Ⓝ

2. Ⓨ Ⓝ

3. Ⓨ Ⓝ

4. Ⓨ Ⓝ

5. Ⓨ Ⓝ

___ / 5 **Total**

There are many different kinds of sandwiches. There are also many different kinds of bread. There are lots of tasty sandwiches. One delicious kind of bread is *pita* (PEE-tuh). Pita is a round, flat bread. It is from the Middle East. But it is very popular all over the world. Pita has a hollow center. When you cut a pita in half, you can fill it. That is why pita is sometimes called *pocket bread*. Another type of bread comes from France. It is called the *baguette* (ba-GET). Baguettes are long, thin loaves of bread. They are crusty on the outside and soft on the inside. Baguettes are great for subs and other long sandwiches. There are many other kinds of bread, too. Which do you like best?

1. Why is pita sometimes called *pocket bread*?

Ⓐ It is from the Middle East.
Ⓑ It is crusty on the outside.
Ⓒ It has a hollow center.
Ⓓ It is flat.

2. Which sentence is **not** true?

Ⓐ Baguettes make very good bread for subs.
Ⓑ Pita comes from France.
Ⓒ Baguettes are long and thin.
Ⓓ A pita is round.

3. Which is **not** a compound word?

Ⓐ outside
Ⓑ inside
Ⓒ sometimes
Ⓓ sandwich

4. Which words are synonyms?

Ⓐ *tasty* and *delicious*
Ⓑ *hollow* and *crusty*
Ⓒ *popular* and *thin*
Ⓓ *pocket* and *center*

5. What is the tone of the text?

Ⓐ informative
Ⓑ comical
Ⓒ opinionated
Ⓓ uncertain

NAME: ______________________ **DATE:** ________________

DIRECTIONS Read the text and then answer the questions.

What is your favorite sandwich? Is it peanut butter and jelly? Is it grilled cheese? Maybe you prefer turkey sandwiches. Sandwiches are popular all over the world. Many tasty sandwiches come from different countries. A *gyro* (YEE-roh) is a Greek sandwich. It is made with pita bread. The pita is filled with beef, lamb, or chicken. It also has lettuce, onion, and tomato. Some people also put sauce on their gyros. A *torta* is a Mexican sandwich. A torta is like a sub. Tortas are made with crusty white rolls. The rolls are filled with meat or fish. They can also have lettuce, beans, tomato, cheese, and avocado. Many people like to put sauce on their tortas.

1. Which title best fits the text?

- Ⓐ Let's Make a Gyro!
- Ⓑ The Story of Mexico
- Ⓒ Bread from All Over
- Ⓓ Sandwiches Around the World

2. *Many tasty sandwiches come from different countries* is which part of the text?

- Ⓐ the title
- Ⓑ the topic sentence
- Ⓒ the setting
- Ⓓ the tone

3. Which words have the same suffix?

- Ⓐ *grilled* and *crusty*
- Ⓑ *filled* and *sandwiches*
- Ⓒ *grilled* and *filled*
- Ⓓ *filled* and *gyros*

4. Which is an antonym of *crusty*?

- Ⓐ soft
- Ⓑ crisp
- Ⓒ long
- Ⓓ sour

5. Which best describes the tone?

- Ⓐ excited
- Ⓑ informative
- Ⓒ indifferent
- Ⓓ defensive

SCORE

1. Ⓨ Ⓝ
2. Ⓨ Ⓝ
3. Ⓨ Ⓝ
4. Ⓨ Ⓝ
5. Ⓨ Ⓝ

___ / 5 **Total**

NAME:______________________ DATE:______________

MAKE YOUR OWN DELICIOUS SANDWICH!

Sandwiches make good lunches and are also easy to make. They can be good for you, too. You can make your own tasty, delicious, mouthwatering sandwich. Here are two recipes. They are both healthy for you, and they taste great! Before you start, be sure an adult is with you and be sure to wash your hands.

Veggie Pita

You will need:

- 1 pita
- 1 slice of cheese
- $\frac{1}{2}$ cup of lettuce
- 1 tomato
- 1 carrot
- falafel *(optional)*
- plain yogurt *(optional)*

Cut the pita in half. Cut the carrot and the tomato into small pieces. Open one half of the pita. Fill it with the cheese, lettuce, tomato, and carrot. Add falafel and yogurt, if you like. Enjoy your creation!

Turkey Baguette

You will need:

- 1 baguette
- 1 leaf of lettuce
- 2 slices of tomato
- 1 slice of onion
- 2 slices of turkey
- mayonnaise or mustard

Cut the baguette in half. Spread the mayonnaise or mustard on the inside. Put the turkey on the baguette. Then, add the onion and the tomato. Then, add the lettuce and close the baguette. Enjoy your sandwich, or share it with a friend—it's your choice!

NAME:____________________________ **DATE:**________________

DIRECTIONS Read "Make Your Own Delicious Sandwich!" and then answer the questions.

1. Which do you need for both the veggie pita and the turkey baguette?

   (A) cheese
   (B) turkey
   (C) mayonnaise
   (D) tomato

2. The purpose is

   (A) to get you to buy something.
   (B) to tell a personal story.
   (C) to tell you how to do something.
   (D) to ask for something.

3. Why would a person make his or her own sandwich?

   (A) Sandwiches are easy to make.
   (B) Sandwiches are healthy.
   (C) Sandwiches taste good.
   (D) all of the above

4. What is the last step in making a turkey baguette?

   (A) closing the baguette
   (B) cutting the baguette in half
   (C) adding the onion
   (D) putting the turkey on the baguette

5. Someone who frequently ______ would best understand the text.

   (A) reads
   (B) cooks
   (C) writes
   (D) instructs

6. What is this text about?

   (A) the history of pita bread
   (B) the history of baguettes
   (C) how to eat healthier
   (D) making pita and baguette sandwiches

SCORE

1. (Y)(N)
2. (Y)(N)
3. (Y)(N)
4. (Y)(N)
5. (Y)(N)
6. (Y)(N)

___ / 6
Total

NAME: ______________________ **DATE:** ______________

DIRECTIONS Reread "Make Your Own Delicious Sandwich!" Then, read the prompt and respond on the lines below.

SCORE
___ / 4

What sandwiches do you like to eat? Write about your favorite sandwiches.

NAME: ______________________ **DATE:** ______________

DIRECTIONS Read the text and then answer the questions.

This was the second science exam that Mike had failed. He was worried, so he decided to ask his science teacher, Mrs. Drake, for help.

"I don't know what I'm doing wrong," he told her. "I feel like a major failure."

"You're not a failure, Mike," Mrs. Drake responded. "You're hardworking and intelligent. Sometimes, people get forgetful when they're nervous, and exams can make people nervous. Is that what's happening to you?"

"Maybe," Mike replied. "Tests definitely make me really nervous."

"Then let's discuss ways to help you feel calm. Maybe that will help."

"Terrific!" Mike said. "Maybe if I feel more relaxed, I'll get higher scores."

1. Which words give an accurate preview of the text?

- Ⓐ *exam*, *worried*, *relaxed*
- Ⓑ *teacher*, *science*, *scores*
- Ⓒ *help*, *failure*, *nervous*
- Ⓓ *sometimes*, *intelligent*, *wrong*

2. What is the setting?

- Ⓐ Mike's home
- Ⓑ Mrs. Drake's home
- Ⓒ a classroom
- Ⓓ the library

3. Which words share a suffix?

- Ⓐ *worried* and *decided*
- Ⓑ *higher* and *calmer*
- Ⓒ *doing* and *hardworking*
- Ⓓ Each word pair shares a suffix.

4. Which is a synonym for *exam*?

- Ⓐ test
- Ⓑ study
- Ⓒ fail
- Ⓓ wrong

5. Which phrase shows that Mike is pleased with Mrs. Drake's suggestion?

- Ⓐ *Tests definitely make me really nervous.*
- Ⓑ *I feel like a major failure.*
- Ⓒ *You're not a failure.*
- Ⓓ *Terrific!*

SCORE

1. Ⓨ Ⓝ
2. Ⓨ Ⓝ
3. Ⓨ Ⓝ
4. Ⓨ Ⓝ
5. Ⓨ Ⓝ

___ / 5 **Total**

NAME: ____________________________ **DATE:** ________________

DIRECTIONS Read the text and then answer the questions.

SCORE

1. Ⓨ Ⓝ
2. Ⓨ Ⓝ
3. Ⓨ Ⓝ
4. Ⓨ Ⓝ
5. Ⓨ Ⓝ

___ / 5
Total

Mike's class was getting ready for an exam about the planets. At first, Mike was worried that he wouldn't do well because exams usually make him nervous. But his science teacher, Mrs. Drake, had taught him several ways to relax. She taught him to breathe deeply. She taught him to look the exam over before starting it. That way, he would know what to expect. She also taught him to read each direction carefully. That way, he would understand what each question was asking. Mrs. Drake's advice really helped! First, Mike took deep breaths. Then, he looked over the exam. All of the questions were about the planets, and he had studied all eight of them. Finally, Mike read the directions carefully. This time, Mike wasn't going to have any problem doing a good job on a science exam!

1. Which title would help a reader preview the text?

Ⓐ Difficult Tests
Ⓑ Test Advice That Works
Ⓒ The Solar System
Ⓓ Deep-Breathing Techniques

2. What is the main problem?

Ⓐ Mike forgot to study for his exam.
Ⓑ Mike gets nervous when he takes exams.
Ⓒ Mike does not like Mrs. Drake.
Ⓓ Mrs. Drake does not like Mike.

3. Which word does **not** have the same root word as *breaths*?

Ⓐ breathe
Ⓑ breathless
Ⓒ breathed
Ⓓ bread

4. A synonym for *carefully* is

Ⓐ quickly.
Ⓑ closely.
Ⓒ slowly.
Ⓓ indifferently.

5. *First*, *then*, and *finally* indicate

Ⓐ the order of events.
Ⓑ the importance of events.
Ⓒ the significance of events.
Ⓓ the meaning of events.

NAME: ______________________ **DATE:** ______________

DIRECTIONS Read the text and then answer the questions.

Mrs. Drake told her science class, "I'm very happy you all did so well on your exams. I'm going to return them to you so you can see for yourselves."

When Mike got his exam, he couldn't believe it! He got a B-plus! He had worked very hard on this exam, and he was excited that he had done so well. He was even more excited when he heard the next thing Mrs. Drake said.

"Since we have been studying the planets, I thought you might like to take a field trip to the planetarium next week! The planetarium has a special room where you will see what the stars and planets look like."

1. Why is Mike excited?

- (A) Mrs. Drake is happy.
- (B) He saw a plane.
- (C) He scored well on his exam.
- (D) He is going to a football game.

2. What is the setting?

- (A) the planetarium
- (B) Mrs. Drake's classroom
- (C) Mike's home
- (D) the school bus

3. Which is the suffix in the word *planetarium*?

- (A) *–tar*
- (B) *planet–*
- (C) *–arium*
- (D) *–net–*

4. Which is defined in the context of the text?

- (A) *planets*
- (B) *stars*
- (C) *planetarium*
- (D) *field*

5. *When Mike got his exam, he couldn't believe it!* is an example of

- (A) a metaphor.
- (B) a simile.
- (C) alliteration.
- (D) hyperbole.

SCORE

1. Ⓨ Ⓝ

2. Ⓨ Ⓝ

3. Ⓨ Ⓝ

4. Ⓨ Ⓝ

5. Ⓨ Ⓝ

___ / 5

Total

NAME: ______________________ **DATE:** ______________

A TRIP TO SEE THE PLANETS

Mike and his science class were taking a field trip to a planetarium. They were going to see what the planets and stars look like. Mike didn't know how they could do that, but he wanted to find out.

All of the students gave their permission slips to their teacher, Mrs. Drake. Then, they got on a bus and went to the planetarium. When they got there, they got off the bus and went inside. Mrs. Drake introduced them to Mrs. Larson. "Mrs. Larson is the director of the planetarium. She will be your tour guide."

Mrs. Larson led the students into a large room full of chairs. She invited everyone to sit down. "Look up at the ceiling," she said. Everyone looked up, but all that the students saw was a big white dome. It certainly wasn't very interesting. "Now, watch what happens," Mrs. Larson said. Then, she pushed a few buttons. Suddenly the lights went off and the dome began to look like a night sky. Mike and his classmates saw the moon and several stars.

"This room has a special ceiling that lets me show you what the sky looks like in different places on Earth and at different times of the year," Mrs. Larson explained. "It also allows me to show you images of the planets." Everyone was fascinated as Mrs. Larson showed the class images of Venus, Saturn, Jupiter, and the other planets. She also showed them different groups of stars.

By the time Mrs. Larson was finished, the students had seen all of the planets they had been studying in class. Mike thought it was so interesting that he began to wonder whether he might enjoy being a scientist. "If this is what scientists get to investigate, I could see myself being one," he thought.

NAME: ______________________ **DATE:** ______________

DIRECTIONS Read “A Trip to See the Planets” and then answer the questions.

1. The title helps the reader predict that the text

(A) will be about a field trip into space.
(B) will be about a field trip to a planetarium.
(C) will be about a field trip to a zoo.
(D) will be about a field trip to Mars.

2. From which point of view is the text written?

(A) third person
(B) first person
(C) second person
(D) multiple points of view

3. Which is **not** true about a planetarium?

(A) It is a building.
(B) It shows pictures of only Venus, Saturn, and Jupiter.
(C) It has a special ceiling.
(D) It displays the night sky.

4. Who is the main character?

(A) Mike's mother
(B) Mrs. Larson
(C) Mrs. Drake
(D) Mike

5. People who like ______ would probably like the text.

(A) art
(B) mathematics
(C) cooking
(D) science

6. What does Mike learn about himself?

(A) He is interested in being a scientist.
(B) He does not want to be a scientist.
(C) He does not like planetariums.
(D) He is afraid of learning about the planets.

SCORE

1. Ⓨ Ⓝ
2. Ⓨ Ⓝ
3. Ⓨ Ⓝ
4. Ⓨ Ⓝ
5. Ⓨ Ⓝ
6. Ⓨ Ⓝ

___ / 6
Total

NAME: ______________________ **DATE:** ______________

DIRECTIONS Reread "A Trip to See the Planets." Then, read the prompt and respond on the lines below.

SCORE

___ / 4

Have you been to a planetarium? What did you think of it? If not, what do you think it would be like?

NAME: ____________________ **DATE:** ____________

DIRECTIONS Read the text and then answer the questions.

SCORE

1. Ⓨ Ⓝ
2. Ⓨ Ⓝ
3. Ⓨ Ⓝ
4. Ⓨ Ⓝ
5. Ⓨ Ⓝ

___ / 5 Total

Do you know who makes our country's laws? Some of the people who make our laws are senators. Each state chooses two senators. Big states choose two senators. So do small states. Senators work for six years. They work to make laws that help the people of their states. They work in Washington, DC. They also work in their home states. To be a senator, a person must be at least thirty years old. A senator must also be a citizen of the United States for at least nine years. Senators must also be residents of their states. That means they must live in the states they represent. Do you know the names of your state's senators?

1. Senators must

Ⓐ choose new senators.
Ⓑ be at least twenty years old.
Ⓒ make twenty laws every year.
Ⓓ be residents of their state.

2. How many senators does each state choose?

Ⓐ six
Ⓑ three
Ⓒ two
Ⓓ five

3. The suffix *–or* tells you that a *senator* is

Ⓐ someone who does something.
Ⓑ a place.
Ⓒ a king.
Ⓓ a way to do something.

4. Which word is defined in the context of the text?

Ⓐ state
Ⓑ residents
Ⓒ laws
Ⓓ citizen

5. Which word best describes the tone?

Ⓐ conversational
Ⓑ sorrowful
Ⓒ comical
Ⓓ upset

NAME:______________________ DATE:________________

SCORE

1. Ⓨ Ⓝ

2. Ⓨ Ⓝ

3. Ⓨ Ⓝ

4. Ⓨ Ⓝ

5. Ⓨ Ⓝ

___ / 5
Total

DIRECTIONS Read the text and then answer the questions.

In which state do you live? Wherever you live, you have a representative. States with a lot of people have lots of representatives. States with smaller populations have fewer representatives. Some states only have one! Representatives work in Washington, DC. They also work in their home districts. Districts are smaller regions of a state. So, a big state has several districts. Representatives work to make laws that will help their districts. They are chosen for two years. They must be at least twenty-five years old. They must also be U.S. citizens for at least seven years. They do not need to live in their districts. But they must live in the same state.

1. States with more ______ have more representatives.

Ⓐ buildings
Ⓑ people
Ⓒ land
Ⓓ money

2. Which is **not** true about representatives?

Ⓐ They are chosen for two years.
Ⓑ They work in Washington, DC.
Ⓒ They must be at least twenty-five years old.
Ⓓ They must live in their districts.

3. Which word makes a new word by adding the suffix *–er*?

Ⓐ have
Ⓑ you
Ⓒ few
Ⓓ live

4. What does *elected* mean?

Ⓐ people
Ⓑ chosen
Ⓒ districts
Ⓓ representatives

5. The phrase *at least twenty-five years old* means

Ⓐ twenty-five and younger
Ⓑ younger than twenty-five
Ⓒ twenty-five and older
Ⓓ older than twenty-five

NAME: ____________________________ **DATE:** ________________

DIRECTIONS Read the text and then answer the questions.

SCORE

1. Ⓨ Ⓝ
2. Ⓨ Ⓝ
3. Ⓨ Ⓝ
4. Ⓨ Ⓝ
5. Ⓨ Ⓝ

___ / 5 Total

Laws are made to help keep people safe. How are laws passed or made? First, a member of Congress creates a bill. Senators are members of Congress. So are representatives. The Senate and the House of Representatives are the two houses of Congress. Any senator or representative can create a bill. Bills are laws that have not been passed yet. After a bill is created, the Senate and the House of Representatives vote on the bill. They decide whether the bill should be a law. If they vote that the bill should not be a law, then it doesn't become a law. If they vote that a bill should be a law, then Congress sends the bill to the president. When the president signs a bill, it becomes a law.

1. What happens if Congress votes that a bill should **not** be a law?

Ⓐ The bill doesn't become a law.
Ⓑ The president signs the bill.
Ⓒ Congress votes on the bill.
Ⓓ The bill is sent to the president.

2. What is the last step in making a law?

Ⓐ A senator or a representative creates a bill.
Ⓑ Congress votes on the bill.
Ⓒ The president signs the bill.
Ⓓ Congress sends the bill to the president.

3. Which words do **not** have the same suffix?

Ⓐ *passed* and *created*
Ⓑ *signs* and *sends*
Ⓒ *vote* and *made*
Ⓓ *laws* and *Representatives*

4. Which is a synonym for *create*?

Ⓐ want
Ⓑ sign
Ⓒ eat
Ⓓ make

5. *Congress creates* is an example of

Ⓐ a hyperbole.
Ⓑ a metaphor.
Ⓒ personification.
Ⓓ alliteration.

NAME:______________________________ DATE:__________________

LET'S VISIT CONGRESS!

The Capitol Building

How does our government work? There are three branches of government. One of those branches is the legislative branch. The verb *legislate* means to make laws. That is one thing this branch does. We call this branch *Congress*. Congress has two houses, or sides. One house is the Senate. There are 100 senators. Why? Each state gets to choose two senators. Senators are chosen for six years.

The other house is the House of Representatives. There are 435 representatives. States with a lot of people have a lot of representatives. States with fewer people do not. Some states only have one. Representatives are chosen for two years. Representatives and senators are members of Congress.

Members of Congress work in the Capitol Building in Washington, DC. One of their jobs is to make laws that will help people. How do they do that? First, a member of Congress creates a bill. Then, Congress votes on whether that bill should be a law. If Congress votes "yes" on the bill, then the bill goes to the president. When the president signs the bill, it becomes a law. If Congress votes "no" on the bill, then it does not become a law.

Congress doesn't just make laws. It is in charge of taxes. It is also in charge of making coins and other money. Congress also makes treaties, or agreements, with other countries. Congress does other things, too. It is an important branch of government.

But Congress can't do whatever it wants to do. There are two other branches of government. Those branches limit what Congress can do. One branch makes sure that the laws Congress creates are fair. The other branches also do other things that Congress cannot do. All three branches have to work together. That way, our government works for everyone.

NAME: ______________________ **DATE:** ______________

DIRECTIONS Read "Let's Visit Congress!" and then answer the questions.

SCORE

1. Which alternative title fits the text?

- (A) Senators and Representatives
- (B) Roots, Branches, and Leaves
- (C) My Day at the Capitol Building
- (D) The House of Representatives

2. A reader would most likely read this text to be

- (A) entertained by facts about the U.S. government.
- (B) informed about the branches of the U.S. government.
- (C) persuaded to run for political office.
- (D) entertained by a fictional trip to the Capitol Building.

3. Why do you think Delaware has only one representative?

- (A) Delaware is near the Atlantic Ocean.
- (B) Delaware is a small state.
- (C) Delaware does not have many people.
- (D) Delaware wants only one representative.

4. What is the first step in making a law?

- (A) A member of Congress creates a bill.
- (B) The president signs the bill.
- (C) Congress sends the bill to the president.
- (D) Congress votes on the bill.

5. Which is **not** true about members of the House of Representatives??

- (A) There are two from each state.
- (B) There are 435 representatives.
- (C) They serve two-year terms.
- (D) They work in the Capitol Building.

6. Why do all three branches of government have to work together?

- (A) Congress can do whatever it wants.
- (B) Each branch can do things that the other branches can't do.
- (C) The president can do anything.
- (D) Each branch is in charge of making laws.

1. Ⓨ Ⓝ
2. Ⓨ Ⓝ
3. Ⓨ Ⓝ
4. Ⓨ Ⓝ
5. Ⓨ Ⓝ
6. Ⓨ Ⓝ

___ / 6
Total

NAME: ______________________ **DATE:** ______________

DIRECTIONS Reread "Let's Visit Congress!" Then, read the prompt and respond on the lines below.

SCORE

___ / 4

If you could create a new law, what would your law be about? Describe your new law and the process it takes to pass the law.

NAME: ______________________ **DATE:** ______________

DIRECTIONS Read the text and then answer the questions.

Rachel searched through her closet for her favorite pair of jeans. Then, she remembered that she had spilled some ketchup on them two days ago. They hadn't been washed yet, and Rachel wanted to wear them the next day. She flopped moodily onto her bed, wondering what else she could wear. Just then, her older brother, Alan, paused as he passed her door.

"What's the matter?" he asked.

"My favorite pair of jeans is dirty and I want to wear them tomorrow. It's annoying!" Rachel said.

"Maybe I can help. If I teach you how to do laundry, you can wash your jeans today and they'll be ready for tomorrow," Alan said. "It's not hard."

"Thanks, Alan!" Rachel said. "Laundry room, here we come!"

1. What is the setting?

Ⓐ school
Ⓑ a restaurant
Ⓒ a house
Ⓓ several different locations

2. What is the character's problem?

Ⓐ ketchup
Ⓑ not being able to wear something
Ⓒ the loss of her pet turtle
Ⓓ an injured leg

3. Which is the suffix in *moodily*?

Ⓐ *–odd*
Ⓑ *mood–*
Ⓒ *–dily*
Ⓓ *–ly*

4. Another word for *annoying* is

Ⓐ frightening.
Ⓑ irritating.
Ⓒ joyful.
Ⓓ sorry.

5. *Laundry room, here we come!* indicates that Rachel is ______ about learning to do laundry.

Ⓐ enthusiastic
Ⓑ upset
Ⓒ surprised
Ⓓ scared

SCORE

1. Ⓨ Ⓝ
2. Ⓨ Ⓝ
3. Ⓨ Ⓝ
4. Ⓨ Ⓝ
5. Ⓨ Ⓝ

___ / 5
Total

NAME: ______________________ **DATE:** ______________

DIRECTIONS Read the text and then answer the questions.

SCORE

1. Ⓨ Ⓝ
2. Ⓨ Ⓝ
3. Ⓨ Ⓝ
4. Ⓨ Ⓝ
5. Ⓨ Ⓝ

___ / 5 Total

Rachel's brother, Alan, was teaching her how to do laundry.

"It's easy to do laundry. First, adjust the washer settings and choose the water temperature," Alan explained. "Cold water helps keep colors bright."

After Rachel set the washer to cold, Alan continued. "Now, you have to set the washer for a small load because you only have one thing to wash."

Rachel set the washer for a small load. Then, Alan said, "Now, put your clothes in and close the washer door. Add some laundry soap, then press the start button. When the washer is finished, we'll put your jeans in the dryer."

Alan was right. Laundry was a piece of cake!

1. This text is

Ⓐ all about soap.

Ⓑ a fictional story about doing laundry.

Ⓒ a detailed account of professional laundry services.

Ⓓ about Alan teaching Rachel how to cook.

2. What does cold water help to do?

Ⓐ keep colors bright

Ⓑ prevent clothes from ripping

Ⓒ create more bubbles

Ⓓ wash clothes faster

3. The word *bright* has

Ⓐ a short vowel.

Ⓑ a long vowel.

Ⓒ a silent vowel.

Ⓓ no vowel.

4. *Easy* and *difficult* are

Ⓐ rhymes.

Ⓑ synonyms.

Ⓒ antonyms.

Ⓓ similes.

5. *Laundry was a piece of cake* is an example of

Ⓐ an onomatopoeia.

Ⓑ an allusion.

Ⓒ hyperbole.

Ⓓ a metaphor.

NAME: ______________________ **DATE:** ______________

DIRECTIONS Read the text and then answer the questions.

Rachel had a surprise for her parents. Her older brother, Alan, had taught her how to do laundry. Now, she could do laundry without any help. One night, Rachel's parents went out to dinner to celebrate their anniversary. As soon as they had gone, Rachel gathered up a pile of dirty towels. She was just putting the towels in the washer when Mom came back in.

"You startled me!" Rachel gasped. "I thought you left!"

"I forgot my cell phone," her mom said. "What are you doing?"

"Alan taught me how to do laundry, and I wanted to surprise you."

"You sure surprised me. What a fabulous anniversary gift!" her mom said.

1. What is Rachel's surprise for her parents' anniversary?

- Ⓐ She cleans up her room.
- Ⓑ She does laundry.
- Ⓒ She makes dinner.
- Ⓓ She buys new towels.

2. What is the problem?

- Ⓐ Mom comes home before Rachel finished doing laundry.
- Ⓑ Rachel doesn't know how to do laundry.
- Ⓒ Rachel can't think of how to surprise her parents.
- Ⓓ Mom doesn't want Rachel to do laundry.

3. What is the root word in *gathered*?

- Ⓐ *there*
- Ⓑ *gather*
- Ⓒ *her*
- Ⓓ *ather*

4. A synonym for *fabulous* is

- Ⓐ wonderful.
- Ⓑ huge.
- Ⓒ expensive.
- Ⓓ funny.

5. Which shows Rachel is surprised?

- Ⓐ said
- Ⓑ gasped
- Ⓒ surprise
- Ⓓ gathered

SCORE

1. ⓎⓃ
2. ⓎⓃ
3. ⓎⓃ
4. ⓎⓃ
5. ⓎⓃ

___ / 5 Total

NAME: ______________________ **DATE:** ______________

A LAUNDRY MYSTERY

When her mom and dad discovered that Rachel had learned to do laundry, they decided to get her a laundry basket. Rachel was pleased about that. It made it easier to get her dirty clothes to the laundry room.

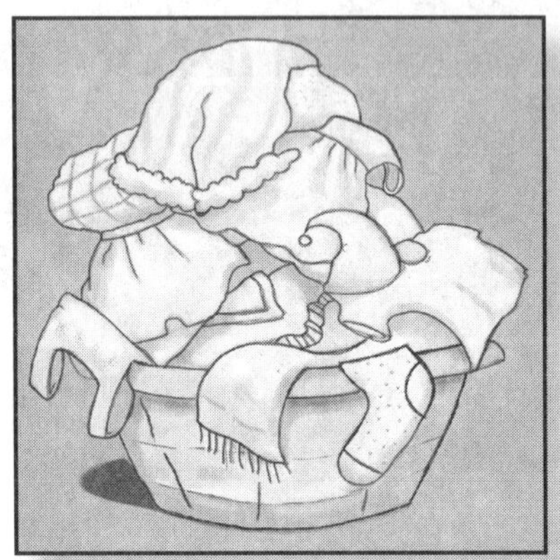

One Saturday afternoon, Rachel noticed that her laundry basket was packed. It was definitely time to wash her clothes. So she dragged her basket to the laundry room and got started. When the washer was finished, she took her clothes out and started putting them into the dryer. Then, she noticed something.

"Mom," she called. "Come here! Quick!"

Her mom came running. "What's the matter, Rachel?"

"Look at this sweater!" Rachel pointed at a pink sweater she was holding. "This isn't supposed to be pink! When we bought it, it was a white sweater! Something happened to it!"

Rachel's mom looked closely at the sweater. Then, she opened the dryer and peered inside at the clothing and other things that Rachel had put in it.

"I think I know what happened," her mom said. "Do you see that red towel?"

Rachel nodded and removed the towel from the dryer. "What about it?"

"That towel is red because it's been dyed that color. And the red dye wasn't colorfast. So some of the red dye rubbed off the towel while it was in the washer and got onto your sweater. When that happens, it's called *bleeding*."

"Then why didn't my sweater turn red?" Rachel wondered aloud.

"Because only some of the dye bled onto the sweater. The rest stayed in the towel."

Rachel thought briefly. Then she said, "Well, I guess it's not horrible that my sweater turned pink. At least it matches some of my other clothes. But I don't want this to happen again."

"The surest way to prevent this problem is to separate the white things from the rest of your laundry. That way, the colored dyes won't mix together among your clothes."

NAME:______________________ **DATE:**______________

DIRECTIONS Read "A Laundry Mystery" and then answer the questions.

1. What is the problem?

- (A) Rachel hates doing laundry.
- (B) Rachel's mom is mad at her.
- (C) Rachel ruins her sweater.
- (D) Rachel is bleeding.

2. A reader would most likely read the text to

- (A) learn how to do laundry.
- (B) learn the meaning of *colorfast*.
- (C) be persuaded to do laundry.
- (D) be entertained by a fictional story.

3. The next time Rachel does her laundry, she will probably

- (A) not go into the laundry room.
- (B) wash her white things separately.
- (C) wash her red towel with her white things.
- (D) buy a pink sweater.

4. By the end of the text, Rachel has learned that

- (A) she should no longer do laundry.
- (B) she needs to wash her clothes according to color.
- (C) she needs to ask permission to wash Mom's clothes.
- (D) fabric dyes turn all clothes red.

5. How does Rachel probably feels when she sees that her sweater is pink?

- (A) grateful
- (B) afraid
- (C) surprised
- (D) delighted

6. Which book title would you expect to have a similar theme?

- (A) Laundry 101
- (B) The Case of the Missing Sock
- (C) The History of Dyeing Fabric
- (D) Colorfast Catastrophes

SCORE

1. (Y)(N)
2. (Y)(N)
3. (Y)(N)
4. (Y)(N)
5. (Y)(N)
6. (Y)(N)

___ / 6
Total

NAME: ______________________ **DATE:** ______________

SCORE

___ / 4

DIRECTIONS Reread “A Laundry Mystery.” Then, read the prompt and respond on the lines below.

Have you ever accidentally dyed your favorite shirt pink? What did you do? If not, what do you imagine it would be like to be in that situation?

NAME: ______________________ **DATE:** ______________

DIRECTIONS Read the text and then answer the questions.

Do you like to go on vacations? Vacations can be relaxing and a lot of fun. You can travel to new places, try new things, and meet new people. But did you know that vacations are good for you? It's true—vacations allow you to rest, and rest is very important because it keeps you healthy. Rest supports your body and your mind by helping you think better and by improving your mood. Vacations provide more than just rest, though. They also allow you to jump, run, swim, and play. Being active is very good for you. When you move your body, you help your body stay healthy. Vacations also let you do things you enjoy. When you do things you enjoy doing, you feel happy, and feeling happy is good for you. So take a vacation!

1. Which title best fits the text?

Ⓐ The Importance of Vacations
Ⓑ Vacation Destinations
Ⓒ Relaxing at Work
Ⓓ Good and Bad Moods

2. What is the main idea?

Ⓐ Being active is healthy.
Ⓑ Vacations are good for you.
Ⓒ Rest helps you think better.
Ⓓ Vacations are a lot of fun.

3. Which is the suffix in *vacation*?

Ⓐ *–on*
Ⓑ *vacate–*
Ⓒ *–tion*
Ⓓ *vaca–*

4. Which words are synonyms?

Ⓐ *rest* and *active*
Ⓑ *mood* and *move*
Ⓒ *also* and *allow*
Ⓓ *rest* and *relax*

5. *Being active is very good for you* should be interpreted

Ⓐ literally.
Ⓑ figuratively.
Ⓒ slowly.
Ⓓ metaphorically.

SCORE

1. Ⓨ Ⓝ
2. Ⓨ Ⓝ
3. Ⓨ Ⓝ
4. Ⓨ Ⓝ
5. Ⓨ Ⓝ

___ / 5
Total

NAME: ____________________ **DATE:** ____________

DIRECTIONS Read the text and then answer the questions.

SCORE

1. Ⓨ Ⓝ
2. Ⓨ Ⓝ
3. Ⓨ Ⓝ
4. Ⓨ Ⓝ
5. Ⓨ Ⓝ

___ / 5
Total

There are many different kinds of vacations. There are many different things to do on vacation. Some people like to be outdoors. Hiking and camping are good vacations for those people. Other people like to go swimming. They like warm weather and sandy beaches. People who like sun, sand, and swimming often go to the ocean. Some people prefer big cities. They like to visit museums and go to restaurants. They like to shop and go to plays and movies. Many people have big families that they like to visit. When they go on vacation, they spend time with their families. What about you? Where do you like to go for vacation?

1. Which sentence gives an accurate preview of the text?

Ⓐ Some people like to be outdoors.

Ⓑ There are many different kinds of vacations.

Ⓒ When they go on vacation, they spend time with their families.

Ⓓ Some people prefer big cities.

2. Which chapter title would help a reader locate the information in the text?

Ⓐ Chapter 5: Vacations in the Big City

Ⓑ Chapter 7: Outdoor Fun

Ⓒ Chapter 3: Choosing the Vacation Destination for You

Ⓓ Chapter 12: Hawaii's Vacation Hot Spots

3. *Swimming*, *hiking*, and *camping* share the same

Ⓐ root word.

Ⓑ prefix.

Ⓒ meaning.

Ⓓ suffix.

4. Which definition of *plays* is used in the text?

Ⓐ dramatic performances

Ⓑ exercise activities

Ⓒ works

Ⓓ amusements

5. *Sun, sand, and swimming* is an example of

Ⓐ alliteration.

Ⓑ a simile.

Ⓒ a rhyme.

Ⓓ a metaphor.

NAME: ______________________ DATE: ______________

DIRECTIONS Read the text and then answer the questions.

SCORE

What should you take with you on vacation? That depends on where you are going. Suppose you are going to the beach. Swimsuits, shorts, and beach towels will be important, and you'll need sunscreen, too. If you are going hiking or camping, you will need different things, such as sturdy, tough shoes, long pants, a jacket, and don't forget the bug spray! Are you going to a big city? Make sure you bring comfortable shoes. You will probably be walking a lot. Where is the city you will be visiting? Find out what the weather is like there. That way, you will be prepared for what kind of clothes to bring. Wherever you go, don't forget a camera so you can take pictures!

1. What should you bring to the big city?

- Ⓐ towels
- Ⓑ comfortable shoes
- Ⓒ long pants
- Ⓓ a jacket

2. What is the main idea?

- Ⓐ You need a swimsuit for a beach vacation.
- Ⓑ If you visit a city, bring comfortable shoes.
- Ⓒ Bring bug spray with you if you go hiking or camping.
- Ⓓ What you need for a vacation depends on where you are going.

3. What is the root word of *comfortable*?

- Ⓐ able
- Ⓑ fort
- Ⓒ comfort
- Ⓓ fortable

4. *Sunscreen* and *outdoors* are

- Ⓐ compound words.
- Ⓑ synonyms.
- Ⓒ antonyms.
- Ⓓ homophones.

5. The language is conversational because

- Ⓐ there are questions in the text to engage the reader.
- Ⓑ a conversation occurs between two characters.
- Ⓒ the author speaks in the text.
- Ⓓ the text is nonfiction.

1. Ⓨ Ⓝ
2. Ⓨ Ⓝ
3. Ⓨ Ⓝ
4. Ⓨ Ⓝ
5. Ⓨ Ⓝ

___ / 5
Total

NAME: ______________________________ **DATE:** ________________

WELCOME ABOARD!

Welcome aboard! You are going on a cruise! A *cruise* is a special kind of vacation on a very large ship. Cruise ships travel to many different places. When you take a cruise, you sleep in a special room called a *cabin*. Cabins are not very big, but they have beds and bathrooms. Most people don't spend very much time in their cabins, though. That is because there is so much to do on a cruise.

Different cruises last for different amounts of time. Some cruises last four days, and others last longer. Some last as long as two weeks. During the cruise, the ship makes stops in different places. You can get off the ship and visit those places while the ship is there. While you are visiting, you can swim, hike, or explore. You can shop, take a walk, try a new activity, or just sit and relax. Then, it is time to get back on board the ship so that it can go to the next place on your cruise. But don't worry—there is so much you can do on a cruise ship that you won't get bored.

Most cruise ships have pools. So you can go swimming on board the ship. Many cruise ships have games and contests you can enter. They also have plays, shows, and other fun activities. Some offer miniature golf and tennis. Some cruise ships even offer rock climbing! You never get hungry on a cruise, either. Cruise ships have several restaurants and other places to eat. No matter what kind of food you like, you'll find it on a cruise ship.

Many people work on the cruise ship to help keep you safe and be sure you have a good time. The captain is in charge of the ship. The cruise director is the person who organizes the activities. There are many other crew members, too. All of them are there to answer questions, make sure the ship is safe, and make sure you enjoy yourself.

NAME: ______________________ **DATE:** ______________

DIRECTIONS Read "Welcome Aboard!" and then answer the questions.

1. Does the title provide enough information to make a prediction about the text?

   - (A) Yes. It tells the reader that the text is about being aboard a train.
   - (B) Yes. It tells the reader that the text is about being aboard cruise ships.
   - (C) No. The text could be about being aboard a train, a ship, or an airplane.
   - (D) No. The text could be about being bored in the car.

2. A reader would most likely read the text to

   - (A) find out what a cruise is like.
   - (B) learn how to play tennis.
   - (C) find out where to go swimming.
   - (D) learn how to become a captain.

3. Most people do not spend time in their ______ even though they sleep in them.

   - (A) hotel rooms
   - (B) bedrooms
   - (C) cabins
   - (D) bedchambers

4. Which sentence is true?

   - (A) All cruises last for one week.
   - (B) Most cruises have one restaurant.
   - (C) Cruises have many games, shows, and activities.
   - (D) The cruise director is in charge of the cruise ship.

5. People who like to ______ will probably enjoy a cruise.

   - (A) be alone
   - (B) rest
   - (C) try new activities
   - (D) play video games

6. Which is **not** something people can do on a cruise ship?

   - (A) shop
   - (B) play tennis
   - (C) swim
   - (D) hike

SCORE

1. Ⓨ Ⓝ
2. Ⓨ Ⓝ
3. Ⓨ Ⓝ
4. Ⓨ Ⓝ
5. Ⓨ Ⓝ
6. Ⓨ Ⓝ

___ / 6 **Total**

NAME: ______________________________ **DATE:** __________________

SCORE

___ / 4

DIRECTIONS Reread "Welcome Aboard!" Then, read the prompt and respond on the lines below.

Have you ever been on a cruise ship? What activities did you do? What activities would you like to do on a cruise ship?

NAME: ______________________ **DATE:** ______________

DIRECTIONS Read the text and then answer the questions.

Daniel sat with the other students in the auditorium. Principal Stephens began to make an announcement.

"Great news. We're going to have a school carnival this year!" he said.

All of the students clapped loudly. They were very excited about the carnival. Mr. Stephens had to ask everyone to be quiet so he could go on.

"Your teacher will tell you more about the carnival. You will find out when and where the carnival will take place. You will also have the chance to share your ideas for the carnival. I hope that everyone will have a good time."

1. Why are the students excited?

Ⓐ Mr. Stephens has to ask everyone to be quiet.

Ⓑ The school is going to have a carnival.

Ⓒ They are in the auditorium.

Ⓓ It is the last day of school.

2. What is the setting?

Ⓐ Mr. Stephen's office

Ⓑ a classroom

Ⓒ the playground

Ⓓ the auditorium

3. What is the root word in *announcement*?

Ⓐ ment

Ⓑ announce

Ⓒ noun

Ⓓ ounce

4. The suffix *–ly* in *loudly* tells the reader about how

Ⓐ the students clapped.

Ⓑ the students cheered.

Ⓒ the principal spoke.

Ⓓ the students spoke.

5. Which phrase shows the students' excitement?

Ⓐ *sat with the other students*

Ⓑ *clapped loudly*

Ⓒ *great news*

Ⓓ *share your ideas for the carnival*

SCORE

1. Ⓨ Ⓝ

2. Ⓨ Ⓝ

3. Ⓨ Ⓝ

4. Ⓨ Ⓝ

5. Ⓨ Ⓝ

___ / 5 Total

NAME: ______________________ **DATE:** ______________

DIRECTIONS Read the text and then answer the questions.

SCORE

1. Ⓨ Ⓝ
2. Ⓨ Ⓝ
3. Ⓨ Ⓝ
4. Ⓨ Ⓝ
5. Ⓨ Ⓝ

___ / 5 Total

Mrs. Blair and her students were discussing the school carnival. Mrs. Blair said, "The theme for our carnival will be the jungle. Decorations will include trees, plants, and animals. What ideas do you have for games and activities?"

Daniel said, "Why don't we have hidden animals? Whoever finds a hidden animal gets a prize."

"That's a terrific idea, Daniel," Mrs. Blair replied. "Now let me hear everyone else's thoughts."

Mrs. Blair soon had a list of great ideas for the carnival!

1. Mrs. Blair and her class are mostly talking about

- Ⓐ hidden animals.
- Ⓑ jungle animals.
- Ⓒ the school carnival.
- Ⓓ balloons and decorations.

2. Which heading best describes the main idea?

- Ⓐ Carnival Decorations
- Ⓑ Planning the School Carnival
- Ⓒ Hidden Animals
- Ⓓ Carnival Activities

3. What suffix can be added to *will* to create a new word?

- Ⓐ *–ing*
- Ⓑ *–est*
- Ⓒ *–able*
- Ⓓ *–ion*

4. Which is a synonym for *hidden*?

- Ⓐ concealed
- Ⓑ exposed
- Ⓒ obvious
- Ⓓ buried

5. Which best describes the tone?

- Ⓐ cheerful
- Ⓑ emotional
- Ⓒ gloomy
- Ⓓ poetic

NAME: ______________________ **DATE:** ______________

DIRECTIONS Read the text and then answer the questions.

SCORE

1. Ⓨ Ⓝ
2. Ⓨ Ⓝ
3. Ⓨ Ⓝ
4. Ⓨ Ⓝ
5. Ⓨ Ⓝ

___ / 5
Total

Come to the Carnival!

Are you ready for a wild good time? Then you won't want to miss our Carnival in the Jungle! There will be hidden jungle animals! There will be face painting and rides! There will be games, prizes, and lots of fun! Snacks and drinks will be available, too! See you there!

Where: Middletown Elementary School

When: Saturday, April 21, from noon to 4:00 P.M.

1. This text is

Ⓐ a recipe.
Ⓑ an invitation.
Ⓒ a newspaper article.
Ⓓ a personal story.

2. Where will the carnival take place?

Ⓐ Middletown Elementary School
Ⓑ Middletown Middle School
Ⓒ Middletown High School
Ⓓ Middletown Public Park

3. Which words do **not** have the same suffix?

Ⓐ *animals* and *rides*
Ⓑ *Saturday* and *Elementary*
Ⓒ *games* and *prizes*
Ⓓ *snacks* and *drinks*

4. Which is a synonym for *available*?

Ⓐ unavailable
Ⓑ inaccessible
Ⓒ accessible
Ⓓ immediate

5. What does the ending punctuation tell the reader about the tone of this text?

Ⓐ It is somber.
Ⓑ It is enthusiastic.
Ⓒ It is formal.
Ⓓ It is apologetic.

NAME: ______________________________ **DATE:** ________________

CARNIVAL TIME!

Daniel and his little sister, Laura, stood in the ticket line at the school carnival. His mom and dad had given Daniel enough money to buy tickets, snacks, and drinks. They were going to park the car. Then, they would come to the carnival, too. Daniel's mom told him, "Stay with your sister. Make sure you two stay together until we get back. I don't want Laura to get lost."

Daniel didn't want Laura to get lost, either. But it wasn't very exciting to go to a carnival with a little kid. Still, he had promised his mom and dad that he would stay with his sister. So Daniel asked, "What do you want to do first, Laura?"

"I want my face painted so I can be a lion," Laura answered.

Daniel and Laura started toward the face-painting booth. The woman at the booth asked what kind of face paint Laura wanted. When Laura told her, she got to work. Laura sat on a stool, pushed her hair away from her face, and closed her eyes.

While Laura was getting her face painted, Daniel looked around at the rest of the activities. Everything looked awesome! He noticed the rides, the food, and the balloons. He wanted to look for hidden animals, too. Everyone who found a hidden animal would win a prize. Daniel was going to ask Laura what she wanted to do next. But when he turned around, Laura had disappeared!

"Laura! Where are you?" Daniel shouted. He was frightened. Where could Laura have gone? His parents would be furious and probably scared, too. "I'm right over here!" someone answered. Daniel looked to his left. Laura was standing right next to a large, decorated tree.

"Don't ever disappear like that again!" Daniel scolded angrily. "You frightened me!"

Laura's lower lip trembled. "I'm sorry," she said. "I thought you saw me. Please don't be mad."

Daniel couldn't stay angry with Laura. After all, she hadn't intended to scare him. He took her hand. "Just don't do it again," he finally said. "Come on, let's get some popcorn."

NAME: ______________________ **DATE:** ______________

DIRECTIONS Read "Carnival Time!" and then answer the questions.

1. Does the title provide enough information to make a prediction about the text?
   - Ⓐ Yes. The text will be about the time a carnival starts.
   - Ⓑ Yes. The text will be about going to the carnival.
   - Ⓒ No. The title is vague, so the text could be about many things.
   - Ⓓ No. The title has nothing to do with the text.

2. From which point of view is the text written?
   - Ⓐ first person
   - Ⓑ second person
   - Ⓒ third person
   - Ⓓ none of the above

3. What frightened Daniel?
   - Ⓐ Laura's painted face
   - Ⓑ the balloon animals
   - Ⓒ Laura's disappearance
   - Ⓓ the rides

4. Who does Daniel have a conflict with?
   - Ⓐ his mom
   - Ⓑ Laura
   - Ⓒ his dad
   - Ⓓ the woman at the face-painting booth

5. Whose situation most closely relates to Daniel's?
   - Ⓐ a boy whose sister copied a friend's homework assignment
   - Ⓑ a babysitter who cannot find the toddler she is responsible for
   - Ⓒ a girl who wanders away from her older brother at an amusement park
   - Ⓓ a parent who has the oldest son babysit their daughter

6. Based on the events in the text, which idiom might Laura want to keep in mind?
   - Ⓐ A penny saved is a penny earned.
   - Ⓑ Curiosity killed the cat.
   - Ⓒ Every cloud has a silver lining.
   - Ⓓ Don't cry over spilled milk.

SCORE

1. Ⓨ Ⓝ
2. Ⓨ Ⓝ
3. Ⓨ Ⓝ
4. Ⓨ Ⓝ
5. Ⓨ Ⓝ
6. Ⓨ Ⓝ

___ / 6

Total

NAME: ______________________ **DATE:** ______________

DIRECTIONS Reread "Carnival Time!" Then, read the prompt and respond on the lines below.

SCORE

___ / 4

If you were Daniel, would you tell your mom and dad that you didn't know where Laura was? Why or why not?

NAME:______________________________ DATE:__________________

DIRECTIONS Read the text and then answer the questions.

Just about everyone goes online. People keep in touch, read news, shop, and get advice online. The Internet started in the 1960s as a business idea. The idea was to link computers so coworkers could share information. The first Internet was called ARPANET. It had thirty-seven linked computers. But there was no World Wide Web yet. That is because computers did not all use the same language. The idea for the Web started in 1980. In the 1980s, three scientists created a special computer language. They wanted all computers to be able to use that language. Then, people could share things with ease. Your computer uses that language. That is how it connects you to the World Wide Web.

1. This text is mostly about

- (A) the first computers.
- (B) a computer language.
- (C) ARPANET.
- (D) the history of the Internet.

2. Which index entry would help a reader locate this information?

- (A) World Wide Web
- (B) ARPANET
- (C) Internet
- (D) all of the above

3. Which prefix makes the antonym of *connect*?

- (A) *pre–*
- (B) *re–*
- (C) *dis–*
- (D) *un–*

4. *Link* and *connect* are

- (A) antonyms.
- (B) synonyms.
- (C) homophones.
- (D) homonyms.

5. What is the author's purpose?

- (A) to entertain
- (B) to instruct
- (C) to inform
- (D) to persuade

SCORE

1. Ⓨ Ⓝ

2. Ⓨ Ⓝ

3. Ⓨ Ⓝ

4. Ⓨ Ⓝ

5. Ⓨ Ⓝ

___ / 5

Total

NAME: ______________________________ **DATE:** ________________

DIRECTIONS Read the text and then answer the questions.

SCORE

1. Ⓨ Ⓝ

2. Ⓨ Ⓝ

3. Ⓨ Ⓝ

4. Ⓨ Ⓝ

5. Ⓨ Ⓝ

___ / 5 **Total**

When you want to play math games, you can go online. But how does that work? How do you get to the math website you want to visit? All computers on the Internet use the same computer language called TCP/IP. When you tell the computer to go to the math website, your computer talks to the math website in TCP/IP. That is how the website knows you want to play a game. When you play a math game, you click or type. Your computer tells the math website what you type or click. It uses TCP/IP to do that. How does your computer know where the website is? Each website has its own address, just as people and businesses do. When you type in the math website's address, the computer finds that place on the World Wide Web.

1. How does a math website know what you type or click?

- Ⓐ You talk to someone at the math website.
- Ⓑ Your computer communicates with the website using TCP/IP.
- Ⓒ The math website reads what you type.
- Ⓓ Your computer tells you what to type or click.

2. Which sentence is the summary sentence?

- Ⓐ the fourth sentence
- Ⓑ the first sentence
- Ⓒ the third sentence
- Ⓓ the second sentence

3. Which syllable is stressed in the word *computer*?

- Ⓐ the first syllable
- Ⓑ the second syllable
- Ⓒ the third syllable
- Ⓓ all of the above

4. Which word has multiple meanings?

- Ⓐ website
- Ⓑ type
- Ⓒ math
- Ⓓ computer

5. *Your computer talks to the math website in TCP/IP* is an example of

- Ⓐ a metaphor.
- Ⓑ personification.
- Ⓒ hyperbole.
- Ⓓ none of the above

NAME: ______________________ **DATE:** ______________

DIRECTIONS Read the text and then answer the questions.

The World Wide Web is a very important part of our lives. Today's World Wide Web lets people do things they could never do before. You can find recipes and advice. You can watch movies and TV shows. You can keep in touch with friends and family. The Internet is also a very good place to find information. Do you want to learn to speak a new language? There are websites that help you learn. There are websites that help you make sure your guitar sounds right. Maybe you want to visit a museum. Many museums have websites that let you take a virtual tour of the museum. The World Wide Web has made it easy to find almost anything you want.

1. Which sentence gives an accurate summary of the text?

- Ⓐ the ninth sentence
- Ⓑ the second sentence
- Ⓒ the sixth sentence
- Ⓓ the last sentence

2. In which chapter would the text be located?

- Ⓐ Chapter 2: Learning Spanish
- Ⓑ Chapter 9: Popular TV Shows
- Ⓒ Chapter 5: Insects
- Ⓓ Chapter 7: The Internet

3. Which vowel sound is **not** in the word *museum*?

- Ⓐ short e
- Ⓑ long e
- Ⓒ short u
- Ⓓ long u

4. What is the tone of the text?

- Ⓐ humorous
- Ⓑ informative
- Ⓒ fearful
- Ⓓ negative

5. Based on the text, the phrase *keep in touch* means

- Ⓐ to touch and then keep items
- Ⓑ to keep items within reach
- Ⓒ to be able to touch an object
- Ⓓ to regularly communicate with others

SCORE

1. Ⓨ Ⓝ

2. Ⓨ Ⓝ

3. Ⓨ Ⓝ

4. Ⓨ Ⓝ

5. Ⓨ Ⓝ

___ / 5
Total

NAME: ______________________ **DATE:** ______________

SURF THE WEB SAFELY!

The World Wide Web can be a lot of fun. It is also a very good place to learn new things. You can play video games, watch your favorite movies, and watch TV shows. You can study, do your homework, and stay in touch with family and friends, too. But it is important to be safe when you use the Internet. Here are some good ways to stay safe when you surf the Web.

Be Private

Never give out your address or phone number online. Do not share your school's name or the name of your sports team, either. Ask your parents before you send a picture of yourself or your family to anyone. Do not give out your friends' addresses or phone numbers. Do not send pictures of your friends to anyone. Do not share passwords; you and your parents are the only people who need to know your password.

Be Polite

Words can hurt, so be polite when you are online. If you wouldn't want anyone to say it to you, don't say it to anyone else. Do not say mean things about people online. Do not take words, pictures, or sounds from a website without permission.

Ask Your Parents

Your parents are there to keep you safe, but they are also there to help you. So show them the websites you visit, talk to them about what you see and do online — and if you get a mean email, tell them about it. It is not your fault if someone sends you something bad. Tell your parents about it. What if someone you don't know wants to meet you? Tell your parents. What if you see something strange on the computer? Tell your parents. Ask your parents before you download anything.

Be safe when you are online. Keep it private, keep it polite, and keep talking to your parents. Happy surfing!

NAME: ______________________ **DATE:** ______________

DIRECTIONS Read "Surf the Web Safely!" and then answer the questions.

1. The title and headings tell readers that they will probably be reading

Ⓐ about how parents are too controlling with video games.

Ⓑ about the Internet, but does not tell the reader anything else.

Ⓒ about parents who like to go to the beach.

Ⓓ about how parents can get involved in Web surfing.

2. What is the purpose for reading this text?

Ⓐ to learn about computers

Ⓑ to learn how to safely use the Internet

Ⓒ to learn about politeness in everyday activities

Ⓓ none of the above

3. People who like ______ would like this text.

Ⓐ the Internet

Ⓑ running

Ⓒ movies

Ⓓ cooking

4. Each paragraph has a heading over it to

Ⓐ tell the reader that those words are not very important.

Ⓑ take up space on the page.

Ⓒ prepare the reader for the main idea of that paragraph.

Ⓓ explain that the Internet is fun.

5. Why should you tell your parents what you see and do online?

Ⓐ Your parents are there to keep you safe and help you.

Ⓑ It is important to be polite.

Ⓒ Do not give out your address or telephone number.

Ⓓ Your parents are not interested in what you do online.

6. Which summarizes the text?

Ⓐ Tell your parents what you see and do online.

Ⓑ Be sure you are polite to your friends when you are online.

Ⓒ Do not give out your address or telephone number.

Ⓓ There are several things you can do to use the Internet safely.

SCORE

1. Ⓨ Ⓝ
2. Ⓨ Ⓝ
3. Ⓨ Ⓝ
4. Ⓨ Ⓝ
5. Ⓨ Ⓝ
6. Ⓨ Ⓝ

___ / 6 Total

NAME: ______________________ **DATE:** ______________

DIRECTIONS Reread "Surf the Web Safely!" Then, read the prompt and respond on the lines below.

SCORE

___ / 4

What are your favorite websites? Write about your favorite websites.

NAME: ______________________ **DATE:** ______________

DIRECTIONS Read the text and then answer the questions.

"I'm going to ride bikes with Eva. I'll be back for dinner," Grace promised Dad.

"Aren't you going to Debbie's birthday party this afternoon?" Dad asked.

Grace looked at the kitchen clock. It was already two o'clock, and the party started at three! She had forgotten all about Debbie's party! "Oh, no!" Grace moaned. "I promised Eva I'd ride bikes with her, and I promised Debbie I'd go to her party! What am I going to do? I can't be in both places."

"If Eva is also invited to the party, then you both can go," suggested Dad.

"Hey, that's a good idea. Maybe Debbie invited Eva, too."

1. Which of the following is an appropriate title for this text?

- (A) Can't Ride a Bike
- (B) One Thing at a Time
- (C) Too Many Promises
- (D) No Friends for Debbie

2. What is Dad's solution to Grace's problem?

- (A) Grace can stay home.
- (B) Grace can call Debbie and tell her she can't come to the party.
- (C) Grace can call Eva and tell her she can't ride bikes.
- (D) Grace and Eva can go to the party together.

3. *I'm* is a contraction of

- (A) *I* and *am*.
- (B) *I* and *will*.
- (C) *I* and *would*.
- (D) *I* and *have*.

4. Which word or phrase is **not** a synonym for *suggested*?

- (A) mentioned
- (B) gained height
- (C) offered advice
- (D) recommended

5. Which of the following is **not** used in the text?

- (A) imagery
- (B) dialogue
- (C) pronouns
- (D) contractions

SCORE

1. Ⓨ Ⓝ

2. Ⓨ Ⓝ

3. Ⓨ Ⓝ

4. Ⓨ Ⓝ

5. Ⓨ Ⓝ

___ / 5 Total

NAME: ____________________ **DATE:** ____________

DIRECTIONS Read the text and then answer the questions.

SCORE

1. Ⓨ Ⓝ

2. Ⓨ Ⓝ

3. Ⓨ Ⓝ

4. Ⓨ Ⓝ

5. Ⓨ Ⓝ

___ / 5 Total

It was a beautiful Wednesday afternoon. Grace was stretched out on the sofa in the living room, chatting with her friend, Eva, on the telephone. Her mom came into the room and waved her hand to get Grace's attention. Then, she pointed to the clock. Grace shook her head and shrugged. She didn't know what her mom meant. Then, her mom pointed to the piano and again at the clock. Now Grace understood what her mom was trying to say.

"I can't believe it!" she said to Eva. "I totally forgot about my piano lesson. I'll call you later, okay?" Grace hung up. She jumped up from the sofa and began flipping through her songbooks. "Sorry, Mom. I'll be ready in a minute," she mumbled. "Why am I always forgetting important things?"

1. Which phrase suggests that someone is relaxing?

Ⓐ *came into the room and waved*
Ⓑ *a beautiful Wednesday*
Ⓒ *was stretched out on the sofa*
Ⓓ *shook her head and shrugged*

2. What is the setting?

Ⓐ the beach
Ⓑ a home
Ⓒ a laundromat
Ⓓ a hotel room

3. The root word in *chatting* is

Ⓐ chatt.
Ⓑ cat.
Ⓒ ting.
Ⓓ chat.

4. In which point of view is this story told?

Ⓐ first person
Ⓑ second person
Ⓒ third person
Ⓓ There is no point of view.

5. Grace has trouble remembering the correct day to do things. Which simile is the **opposite** of how Grace should be described?

Ⓐ Grace is like a kite.
Ⓑ Grace is like a lion.
Ⓒ Grace is like a fortress.
Ⓓ Grace is like a calendar.

NAME: ______________________ **DATE:** ______________

DIRECTIONS Read the text and then answer the questions.

"All right, everyone," Mrs. Wilson announced. "Please put your books and notebooks away. I'll hand out the exam now, and you may begin."

"Exam?" Grace hissed to Marie, who was sitting beside her.

"Of course, exam!" Marie whispered. "Don't you remember? Mrs. Wilson wrote it on the board last week and reminded us about it two days ago."

"I forgot about the exam. What am I supposed to do now?"

"Just do the best you can," Mrs. Wilson said. She had been listening to the girls' conversation. "We'll discuss it after class."

1. Which phrase indicates the setting of this text?

- (A) *all right, everyone*
- (B) *hand out the exam*
- (C) *Mrs. Wilson*
- (D) *wrote it on the board*

2. What is Grace's problem?

- (A) Marie is mad at her.
- (B) She forgot about a test.
- (C) She was caught gossiping.
- (D) She got in trouble for eavesdropping.

3. Which is the root word in the word *conversation*?

- (A) con
- (B) conver
- (C) converse
- (D) none of the above

4. Based on the text's use of the word *conversation*, *converse* probably means

- (A) to repair or fix a broken item.
- (B) a cool shoe worn for basketball.
- (C) a game played for exercise.
- (D) social interaction through speech.

5. The words *hissed* and *whispered* indicate that Grace is

- (A) talking on a telephone.
- (B) singing.
- (C) yelling.
- (D) trying to be quiet.

SCORE

1. Ⓨ Ⓝ
2. Ⓨ Ⓝ
3. Ⓨ Ⓝ
4. Ⓨ Ⓝ
5. Ⓨ Ⓝ

___ / 5 **Total**

NAME: ______________________ **DATE:** ______________

TIME TO GET ORGANIZED!

Grace knew she needed to talk to her teacher, Mrs. Wilson. She was having trouble in class, and it was mostly because she kept forgetting things. After class, Grace waited until everyone had left and then approached Mrs. Wilson's desk.

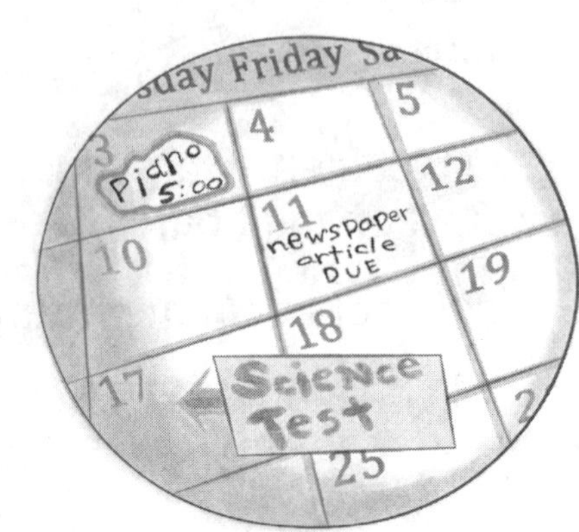

"I know I did really badly on the exam today," Grace began. "I could have done a whole lot better."

"What do you think happened?" Mrs. Wilson asked. She wanted to get Grace's point of view.

"I think it's because I keep forgetting things. I forgot we were having an exam today, so I didn't think about studying like I usually do. That happens to me a lot because I do a lot of things. Keeping everything organized is really hard for me."

"What other things do you do?" Mrs. Wilson wanted to know.

"Well, there's school, and I take piano lessons, so I have to practice the piano every day. I also write articles for the school newspaper. And I want to have fun with my friends, too."

"It sounds like you're busy, but that doesn't mean you can't get organized. What you need to do is manage your time better," Mrs. Wilson said.

"That's what my parents tell me, too," Grace said with a sigh.

"Well, they're right," Mrs. Wilson said. "And you can begin getting organized by getting a calendar. If you get a large calendar, you can write down everything you need to do. Then every day, you can check your calendar to see what's on your schedule."

Grace was beginning to get the idea. "And I can write my assignments and tests on my calendar, too, so I don't forget to study!"

"Exactly!" Mrs. Wilson said. "If you know you have an exam in a week, you can begin studying a little each day. That way, you'll be prepared for the exam, but you'll still have time for other things."

"Thanks, Mrs. Wilson," Grace smiled. "I guess I should have paid attention to my parents in the first place."

NAME: ______________________ DATE: ______________

DIRECTIONS Read "Time to Get Organized!" and then answer the questions.

1. After reading this text, a reader will be able to

- Ⓐ explain why organization is important.
- Ⓑ explain what a calendar is.
- Ⓒ talk about classrooms.
- Ⓓ warn students about exams and how hard they are.

2. The author most likely wrote this to

- Ⓐ entertain readers so that they will want to read more.
- Ⓑ inform readers on proper classroom behavior.
- Ⓒ persuade readers to learn about calendars.
- Ⓓ persuade readers to become organized.

3. What might happen if Grace gets a calendar?

- Ⓐ Grace will do badly on all her tests.
- Ⓑ Grace will not forget to do things.
- Ⓒ Grace's parents will be angry with her.
- Ⓓ Mrs. Wilson will get Grace a calendar.

4. If Grace studies a little every day, she will

- Ⓐ forget everything.
- Ⓑ be ready for the exam and still have time for other things.
- Ⓒ take piano lessons and practice every day.
- Ⓓ write everything on her calendar.

5. Which would best help Grace to become organized?

- Ⓐ a computer with a digital calendar
- Ⓑ a computer for playing video games
- Ⓒ talking to Mrs. Wilson each night about homework
- Ⓓ none of the above

6. Grace is most similar to the hare in "The Tortoise and the Hare" because

- Ⓐ she knows what to do.
- Ⓑ she is slow but always finishes.
- Ⓒ she is disorganized but very quick.
- Ⓓ her lack of planning causes her to do poorly.

SCORE

1. Ⓨ Ⓝ
2. Ⓨ Ⓝ
3. Ⓨ Ⓝ
4. Ⓨ Ⓝ
5. Ⓨ Ⓝ
6. Ⓨ Ⓝ

___ / 6 Total

NAME: ______________________ **DATE:** ______________

SCORE

___ / 4

DIRECTIONS Reread "Time to Get Organized!" Then, read the prompt and respond on the lines below.

What do you do each day? Write your schedule for one or two days.

NAME: ______________________ **DATE:** ________________

DIRECTIONS Read the text and then answer the questions.

Bull's-eye! An arrow whistles through the air! It hits the target! Bows and arrows are beautiful to watch. They are useful, too. Bows and arrows have a very long history. Early humans made the first arrows from wood. They burnt the wood and then sharpened it into points. Later, people made arrows with stone tips. The bow and arrow made it much easier to hunt. Before the bow and arrow, hunters had to use sharpened sticks. Sometimes, they used spears. But a hunter had to get very close to a wild animal to use a stick or spear, which was dangerous. A bow and arrow were safer. They let the hunter stay far away from the prey. Today, some people still go hunting. Sometimes, they use bows and arrows.

1. Why was it dangerous to hunt with a spear?

- Ⓐ Spears could be thrown from far away.
- Ⓑ Spears were faster.
- Ⓒ Spears were louder.
- Ⓓ Hunters sometimes needed to get close to wild animals.

2. Which title most appropriately describes the text?

- Ⓐ The History of the Bow and Arrow
- Ⓑ How to Hunt Large Animals
- Ⓒ Collecting Stone-Age Artifacts
- Ⓓ Bull's-Eye!

3. Which shows the correct pronunciation of *sharpened*?

- Ⓐ shahr-PUHN-ed
- Ⓑ shahr-PUHND
- Ⓒ SHAHR-puhn-ed
- Ⓓ SHAHR-puhnd

4. Which is a synonym for *dangerous*?

- Ⓐ secure
- Ⓑ risky
- Ⓒ enormous
- Ⓓ nervous

5. *An arrow whistles through the air!* The word *whistles* tells about

- Ⓐ the size of the arrow.
- Ⓑ the color of the arrow.
- Ⓒ the speed of the arrow.
- Ⓓ the noise the arrow makes.

SCORE

1. Ⓨ Ⓝ
2. Ⓨ Ⓝ
3. Ⓨ Ⓝ
4. Ⓨ Ⓝ
5. Ⓨ Ⓝ

___ / 5

Total

NAME: ______________________ **DATE:** ______________

DIRECTIONS Read the text and then answer the questions.

SCORE

1. Ⓨ Ⓝ
2. Ⓨ Ⓝ
3. Ⓨ Ⓝ
4. Ⓨ Ⓝ
5. Ⓨ Ⓝ

___ / 5
Total

Arrows look very simple, but they are made of several parts that all have to work together. The *arrowhead* is the sharpened point of the arrow. That is what hits the target or the prey. The arrowhead is connected to a shaft. The *shaft* of an arrow is the long, straight part of the arrow. Along the shaft is called *fletching*. Fletching is the group of plastic feathers you see on arrows. Fletching gives the arrow balance and helps it move in a straight line. At the very end of the shaft is the *nock*. The nock is a little plastic slot that is used to fit the arrow into the string of a bow. Some arrows are made of wood. But many are made of aluminum (uh-LOO-muh-nuhm). Aluminum is the same metal used in making cans.

1. What would clarify the parts of an arrow described in this text?

- Ⓐ a glossary definition
- Ⓑ a thesaurus
- Ⓒ a friend who is an archer
- Ⓓ a labeled diagram of an arrow

2. Which can be used to find the meaning of the word *fletching*?

- Ⓐ the Internet
- Ⓑ a glossary
- Ⓒ a dictionary
- Ⓓ all of the above

3. Which syllable is stressed in the word *aluminum*?

- Ⓐ the first syllable
- Ⓑ the second syllable
- Ⓒ the third syllable
- Ⓓ the fourth syllable

4. Which is a synonym for *connected*?

- Ⓐ apart
- Ⓑ joined
- Ⓒ next to
- Ⓓ larger

5. What is the author's purpose?

- Ⓐ to inform
- Ⓑ to persuade
- Ⓒ to instruct
- Ⓓ to explain

NAME: ______________________ **DATE:** ______________

DIRECTIONS Read the text and then answer the questions.

What happens when you shoot an arrow? How does it get to its target? First, you fit the arrow onto the string of the bow. Then, you draw the string back towards you. When you do that, you are storing energy that you will use to shoot the arrow. Then, you shoot the arrow. When you do that, the energy you stored moves to the arrow and pushes it. When you shoot an arrow, it doesn't fly perfectly straight. An arrow actually flies in an arch pattern, which is why people who shoot arrows are called *archers*. At first, the arrow goes up because of the force used to shoot. But gravity pulls the arrow back down. If you use enough force, the arrow will hit the target before it hits the ground.

1. What are people who shoot arrows called?

- (A) shooters
- (B) archers
- (C) arrowers
- (D) forcers

2. What pulls an arrow down?

- (A) push
- (B) pull
- (C) gravity
- (D) the ground

3. Which word has the same root word as *archers*?

- (A) parched
- (B) arrow
- (C) ranch
- (D) archery

4. In this text, what does *draw* mean?

- (A) sketch
- (B) an even score
- (C) pull
- (D) lengthen

5. The word *actually* implies

- (A) that arrows fly low to the ground before they hit their target.
- (B) that the reader may think arrows don't fly in an arch.
- (C) that arrows act like an arch.
- (D) that arrows are exciting and fun to hunt with.

SCORE

1. Ⓨ Ⓝ
2. Ⓨ Ⓝ
3. Ⓨ Ⓝ
4. Ⓨ Ⓝ
5. Ⓨ Ⓝ

___ / 5
Total

NAME: ______________________ **DATE:** ____________

BULL'S-EYE!

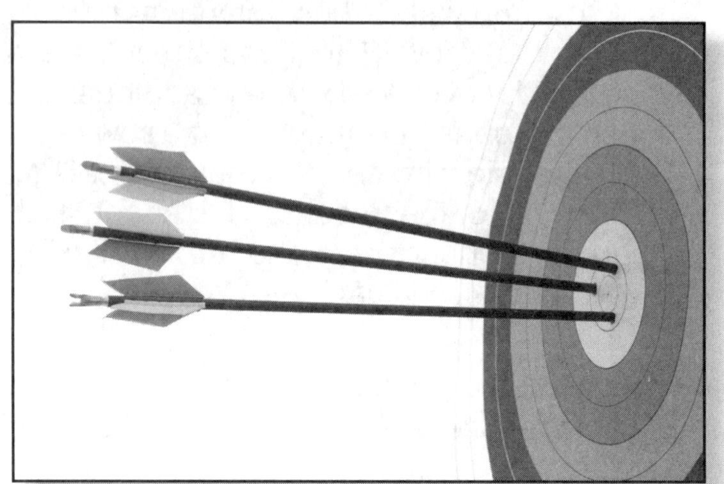

Have you ever wondered what it would be like to use a bow and arrow? People have used bows and arrows for thousands of years. Many people still do use bows and arrows. Archery—shooting arrows—is a very popular sport. It is even an Olympic event! People love to see their arrows hit the middle of the target. That is called *hitting the bull's-eye*. Archery is also a safe sport. It is safer than sports like baseball and football where balls are used.

Archery is good for your body. When you shoot arrows, you use your upper body. Using your body helps to keep it strong. Shooting arrows also helps your mind, too. How? In archery, you must keep your mind on what you are doing. You must block out other things. When you do that, you learn to focus. Being able to focus helps you think better.

Almost anyone can learn archery. You do not have to be very big or strong. So archery is a good sport for a lot of people. You do not have to buy expensive bows and arrows. You can rent bows and arrows from an archery club. Many clubs offer lessons, too. So even if you are a beginner, you can learn. You can take lessons with other kids, too, and make new friends.

Archery is a safe and fun sport. But you still need to be careful. Take lessons from an expert. Make sure you have an adult with you when you are practicing. It is also important to shoot in a safe place. Most archery clubs have safe places for practicing. You can practice there without hurting anyone. When you are at the club, follow all of the rules; they are there to keep you safe. It is also important to use safe equipment. Make sure your bows and arrows are in good shape. If you do it safely, archery can be a lot of fun. So be safe, have fun, and hit that bull's-eye!

NAME: ______________________ **DATE:** ______________

DIRECTIONS Read "Bull's-Eye!" and then answer the questions.

1. Based on the title alone, a reader might think this is about

- (A) target shooting.
- (B) archery.
- (C) darts.
- (D) all of the above

2. The author probably wrote this to

- (A) warn of how incredibly dangerous archery can be.
- (B) introduce a fun sport.
- (C) help get an archery business going.
- (D) all of the above

3. Why is archery good for your body?

- (A) It helps your eyesight improve.
- (B) It helps you make friends.
- (C) It is a form of exercise.
- (D) It doesn't take too much thinking.

4. Which is **not** true about archery?

- (A) It helps you focus.
- (B) There are no rules.
- (C) It is a safe sport.
- (D) It is an Olympic event.

5. Based on your knowledge of other sports, which of the following will **not** help an athlete in archery?

- (A) safe, well-built equipment
- (B) an archery instructor
- (C) cool shoes with stripes
- (D) an archery range

6. Which is the best summary of this text?

- (A) Archery is a safe sport. It is safer than sports that use balls.
- (B) People like archery because they love to see their arrows hit the bull's-eye.
- (C) If you are careful, archery is a fun and safe sport that is also good for you.
- (D) Archery clubs have safe places to practice shooting.

SCORE

1. Ⓨ Ⓝ
2. Ⓨ Ⓝ
3. Ⓨ Ⓝ
4. Ⓨ Ⓝ
5. Ⓨ Ⓝ
6. Ⓨ Ⓝ

___ / 6
Total

NAME: ______________________ **DATE:** ______________

DIRECTIONS Reread "Bull's-Eye!" Then, read the prompt and respond on the lines below.

SCORE

___ / 4

What do you think you would like about archery? What would you not like? Write about what you would like and not like.

NAME: ______________________________ **DATE:** __________________

DIRECTIONS Read the text and then answer the questions.

Steve and his class were learning about the pioneers. Mr. Jacobs showed a documentary about pioneers. Before Mr. Jacobs started the film, he said, "This film doesn't show real pioneers. There was no way to make movies at the time they lived. But you will see the kinds of homes they had. You will also see the kinds of food they ate and their clothes." When the documentary was over, Mr. Jacobs asked if anyone had questions.

"Pioneers made everything by hand? Wasn't that hard?" Steve asked.

"It was very hard, Steve," Mr. Jacobs answered. "Pioneer living was extremely difficult. Pioneers didn't have as many machines as we do now. They had some tools, but they weren't as useful as the ones we have today."

1. Which image would best support the text?

- (A) a pioneer playing video games
- (B) a pioneer waving to a crowd
- (C) a pioneer making butter by hand
- (D) a pioneer using a washing machine

2. Why doesn't the film show real pioneers?

- (A) Films didn't exist during the time of pioneers.
- (B) Pioneers were too shy to be recorded.
- (C) Mr. Jacobs doesn't like pioneers.
- (D) Real pioneers are boring.

3. Which syllable is stressed in the word *documentary*?

- (A) the first syllable
- (B) the second syllable
- (C) the third syllable
- (D) the fourth syllable

4. Another word for *extremely* is

- (A) someone.
- (B) many.
- (C) very.
- (D) never.

5. The antonym of *started* is

- (A) tried.
- (B) began.
- (C) finished.
- (D) offered.

SCORE

1. Ⓨ Ⓝ

2. Ⓨ Ⓝ

3. Ⓨ Ⓝ

4. Ⓨ Ⓝ

5. Ⓨ Ⓝ

___ / 5

Total

NAME: ____________________________ **DATE:** ________________

DIRECTIONS Read the text and then answer the questions.

SCORE

1. Ⓨ Ⓝ

2. Ⓨ Ⓝ

3. Ⓨ Ⓝ

4. Ⓨ Ⓝ

5. Ⓨ Ⓝ

___ / 5 Total

Steve and his classmates were working on their pioneer project. Each group in the class was planning a journey in a covered wagon. The groups' assignment was to make a list of things to take. The wagons couldn't hold everything, so they had to choose carefully. Also, nobody was allowed to include things pioneers wouldn't have had.

"Are we bringing enough food? Pioneers traveled for months," Nick said.

"Nick's right," Steve added. "We need to include a ton of food supplies."

"But we don't have enough room in the wagon for any more food," Jessica pointed out. "Hunting and fishing tools take up less room than food does. Our pioneers will have enough to eat if they can hunt and fish on the way."

1. The first sentence suggests that the text takes place

Ⓐ at school.

Ⓑ in a restaurant.

Ⓒ at a party.

Ⓓ at a doctor's office.

2. Steve's group must decide

Ⓐ whether to bring a cell phone or a radio.

Ⓑ who gets to travel in a covered wagon.

Ⓒ who drives a covered wagon.

Ⓓ what to bring on a trip in a covered wagon.

3. The root word in *assignment* is

Ⓐ men.

Ⓑ meant.

Ⓒ assign.

Ⓓ ment.

4. A synonym for *thing* is

Ⓐ person.

Ⓑ item.

Ⓒ bag.

Ⓓ wagon.

5. *We need to include a ton of food supplies* uses

Ⓐ imagery.

Ⓑ personification.

Ⓒ hyperbole.

Ⓓ rhythm.

NAME: ______________________ **DATE:** ______________

DIRECTIONS Read the text and then answer the questions.

Steve's class was getting ready for a field trip to Pioneer Village. The class had been studying pioneers in school. Today, they were going to see a special small town. It was built exactly like a pioneer town.

Steve got his things together and put them in his backpack. He packed his sunglasses and a hat. He also packed his digital camera. "I wonder if I'm forgetting anything," Steve thought. Then he remembered something he wanted. He got out a sweatshirt and put it in his backpack.

"Now I have everything I need," Steve thought. "Pioneers didn't have sunglasses, cameras, or sweatshirts. And I'm riding on a bus, not a covered wagon. But it will still be fun to see what it was like to be a pioneer."

1. What is the text about?

- (A) practicing to be a pioneer
- (B) preparing for a field trip to Pioneer Village
- (C) riding on a bus
- (D) forgetting to pack a sweatshirt

2. The dialogue in the story shows that Steve is

- (A) a pioneer.
- (B) careless.
- (C) really into music.
- (D) thoughtful.

3. Which is **not** a compound word?

- (A) something
- (B) sweatshirts
- (C) sunglasses
- (D) camera

4. The antonym of *everything* is

- (A) something.
- (B) nothing.
- (C) anything.
- (D) everyone.

5. What is the tone of the text?

- (A) bored
- (B) excited
- (C) alarmed
- (D) contemplative

SCORE

1. Ⓨ Ⓝ
2. Ⓨ Ⓝ
3. Ⓨ Ⓝ
4. Ⓨ Ⓝ
5. Ⓨ Ⓝ

___ / 5 Total

NAME:_______________________________ DATE:__________________

WHAT A FIELD TRIP!

Steve's class arrived at Pioneer Village at ten o'clock. A tour guide greeted them. "Hello, everyone, and welcome to Pioneer Village. I am Mrs. Hendricks, your guide. I hope everyone will have a terrific visit."

Soon the class began to explore. It looked exactly like a pioneer town. There were no malls or pizza restaurants. Instead, there was a general store where you could purchase clothes, tools, and dishes. You could also get flour, sugar, and other things. There was a schoolhouse, too, but it didn't resemble Steve's school. It definitely looked like a classroom, though. There were desks for the teacher and students. There was also a blackboard.

For Steve, the best building in Pioneer Village was the jailhouse. The jailhouse had a sheriff's office and some small jail cells. Steve's class had seen this kind of jail in the documentary his teacher had shown them. Steve didn't imagine it would be very much fun being a real prisoner, but he had fun exploring. He enjoyed it so much that when everyone else left to go to another building, he stayed behind. He had just entered one of the cells to look around when he heard a loud bang behind him. The cell door had slammed shut! Steve rattled the door, but it wouldn't budge.

When Steve realized he was trapped, he began shouting, "Help me! I'm stuck in this jail cell!" Suddenly he heard footsteps running up the steps to the jailhouse. The door swung open and Steve saw to his relief that his teacher, Mr. Jacobs, was there. Mr. Jacobs was with the sheriff who had shown the class the jailhouse.

"Just a second and I'll have you out," said the sheriff. "That door sticks, and it's really difficult to open it from the inside." In a minute, he had gotten the door open and Steve was free.

"I've definitely learned one thing," Steve remarked after he'd thanked the sheriff. "I never want to go to jail for real!"

NAME: ______________________ **DATE:** ______________

DIRECTIONS Read "What a Field Trip!" and then answer the questions.

1. The title suggests that the text will be about

Ⓐ aircraft carriers and the planes they have.
Ⓑ a trip to a field of flowers.
Ⓒ a regular, uninteresting field trip.
Ⓓ none of the above

2. The purpose for reading this text is

Ⓐ for entertainment through a first-person narrative.
Ⓑ for entertainment through a third-person narrative.
Ⓒ to gather information.
Ⓓ to learn about different opinions.

3. Which is **not** at Pioneer Village?

Ⓐ a general store
Ⓑ a schoolhouse
Ⓒ a jailhouse
Ⓓ a cell phone store

4. How does Mr. Jacobs probably feel when Steve gets stuck?

Ⓐ jealous
Ⓑ afraid
Ⓒ proud
Ⓓ worried

5. What did the pioneer classroom not have?

Ⓐ desks
Ⓑ computers
Ⓒ seats
Ⓓ a door

6. Steve getting stuck in the jail cell is an example of

Ⓐ a character working with a team to solve a conflict.
Ⓑ a character solving a conflict.
Ⓒ a character encountering a conflict.
Ⓓ all of the above

SCORE

1. Ⓨ Ⓝ
2. Ⓨ Ⓝ
3. Ⓨ Ⓝ
4. Ⓨ Ⓝ
5. Ⓨ Ⓝ
6. Ⓨ Ⓝ

___ / 6 Total

NAME: ______________________ **DATE:** ______________

SCORE

___ / 4

DIRECTIONS Reread "What a Field Trip!" Then, read the prompt and respond on the lines below.

What do you think your life would be like if you were a pioneer? Write about what your life would be like.

NAME:______________________ DATE:______________

DIRECTIONS Read the text and then answer the questions.

As we learn more about our world, we understand it better. And when we learn more about something, we are often less afraid of it. For example, when cars were first invented, many people were afraid of them. They didn't want to ride in cars. But we have since learned a lot about cars and now understand them better. So most people have stopped being afraid of them. The same thing is true of electricity. In the early 1800s, many people were afraid of electricity. They didn't know how it worked. That made them afraid. Today, we know a lot about electricity. We know how it works, so most people are not afraid of it. If you use it safely, it won't hurt you. The more you know about things, the less scary those things are.

1. The first two sentences indicate that the text is about

Ⓐ fear and how the world is really large.

Ⓑ fear and how it is unstoppable.

Ⓒ fear and overcoming it through knowledge.

Ⓓ fear and why parachuting is scary.

2. Which of these could be a summary sentence of the text?

Ⓐ As we learn more about things, we become less afraid of them.

Ⓑ As we discover electricity, we slowly drive our cars better.

Ⓒ People drove scary cars in the 1800s, but now they do not.

Ⓓ The more we learn about things, the better.

3. Which is the root of *electricity*?

Ⓐ electrical

Ⓑ elec

Ⓒ electric

Ⓓ ele

4. Another word for *scary* is

Ⓐ boiling.

Ⓑ infuriating.

Ⓒ boring.

Ⓓ frightening.

5. What is the author's purpose?

Ⓐ to ask questions about fear and investigate how it can be fun

Ⓑ to explain a method for overcoming fear

Ⓒ to argue that driving is scary

Ⓓ to allow for the dispersal of electricity

SCORE

1. Ⓨ Ⓝ

2. Ⓨ Ⓝ

3. Ⓨ Ⓝ

4. Ⓨ Ⓝ

5. Ⓨ Ⓝ

___ / 5 Total

NAME: ______________________ **DATE:** ______________

DIRECTIONS Read the text and then answer the questions.

SCORE

1. Ⓨ Ⓝ

2. Ⓨ Ⓝ

3. Ⓨ Ⓝ

4. Ⓨ Ⓝ

5. Ⓨ Ⓝ

___ / 5

Total

Life was very different in the early 1800s. For example, people did not have automobiles or trains. In the early 1800s, they rode on horses or in carriages. At that time, people didn't have electricity. Most people used candles and fireplaces to give them light and heat. With the invention of the steam engine, machines could make things faster and easier. There were factories, too. They used steam power. Some people at that time were very, very rich. Life was good for the wealthy. But most people were not wealthy. In fact, over half of England's people were poor. Life was very hard for them. Many poor people, even children, worked in factories. Yet the factories were not safe; many people who worked in factories got hurt, and some even died.

1. Which image would best help a reader preview the text?

   Ⓐ a map of England in the 1800s

   Ⓑ a diagram of an old train

   Ⓒ a picture of kids playing in the 1800s

   Ⓓ a picture of a factory in the 1800s

2. Which is **not** a way life was different in the early 1800s?

   Ⓐ There were no cars.

   Ⓑ People had fireplaces.

   Ⓒ There was no electricity.

   Ⓓ There were no trains.

3. The root word in *wealthy* is

   Ⓐ weal.

   Ⓑ we.

   Ⓒ wealth.

   Ⓓ healthy.

4. A synonym for *automobile* is

   Ⓐ engine.

   Ⓑ mobile.

   Ⓒ train.

   Ⓓ car.

5. To create hyperbole, which could replace *very, very rich*?

   Ⓐ infinitely rich

   Ⓑ somewhat rich

   Ⓒ rich, but only a little

   Ⓓ very rich

NAME: ____________________ **DATE:** ______________

DIRECTIONS Read the text and then answer the questions.

In the early 1800s, life was changing very fast. Many people moved from farms to cities. People started to work in factories. Many people didn't like the big changes. They saw that there was a lot of sickness, pollution, and poverty. They thought life was becoming too dangerous and stressful. These people thought that humans had gone too far with technology. They were afraid of what would happen if there were any more machines. One woman wrote a book about this. Her name was Mary Shelley. Her book was called *Frankenstein* (FRANG-kuhn-stahyn). The book is about a man who makes a new creature. But when he sees what he has done, he realizes he has gone too far. The book became very popular. It is sometimes called the first science-fiction novel.

1. Which literary genre is *Frankenstein*?

Ⓐ nonfiction
Ⓑ science fiction
Ⓒ realistic fiction
Ⓓ fairy tale

2. How did many people feel about the changes of the early 1800s?

Ⓐ happy
Ⓑ excited
Ⓒ bored
Ⓓ afraid

3. How many syllables are in the word *Frankenstein*?

Ⓐ one syllable
Ⓑ two syllables
Ⓒ three syllables
Ⓓ four syllables

4. A *novel* is a kind of

Ⓐ recipe.
Ⓑ book.
Ⓒ machine.
Ⓓ person.

5. Comparing technology to a monster is an example of

Ⓐ imagery.
Ⓑ a metaphor.
Ⓒ alliteration.
Ⓓ onomatopoeia.

SCORE

1. Ⓨ Ⓝ
2. Ⓨ Ⓝ
3. Ⓨ Ⓝ
4. Ⓨ Ⓝ
5. Ⓨ Ⓝ

___ / 5
Total

NAME: ______________________ **DATE:** ______________

MARY SHELLEY

Mary Shelley

Mary Shelley was born on August 30, 1797. Her mother died soon after she was born, so Mary was raised by her father, William. Four years later, William married again. William's new wife, Mary Jane, had children of her own. So Mary grew up with four brothers and sisters.

William was friends with many great scientists, poets, and writers. Mary grew up with books, poems, and ideas. Mary was also lucky in another way. At the time she was growing up, girls usually did not go to school. But William thought that girls should learn just the same way boys did. So Mary got a good education.

One of William's friends was a poet. His name was Percy Shelley. Percy and Mary became friends and then fell in love. They got married when Mary was only sixteen. In the summer of 1816, Mary and Percy took a trip with some friends. The weather was bad, so the group had to stay inside. One day, they decided to see who could write the best ghost story. Mary's idea for a story came to her in a dream. She would write a story about a man who wanted to create a new creature. But when he saw what he made, he realized he had gone too far. Mary's story was very scary. Everyone agreed that Mary's was the best ghost story.

Two years later, that story was made into a book called *Frankenstein*. The book became popular right away. At eighteen, Mary Shelley was a famous writer! Her book made people think a lot. It was also a good scary story. Mary wrote other books, too. She and Percy also had two children, Clara and William. After a few years, the family moved to Italy. There, Percy became a very famous poet. Sadly, Percy died in Italy. Mary went back to England with her children. She died there in 1851.

NAME: ______________________ DATE: ______________

DIRECTIONS Read “Mary Shelley” and then answer the questions.

1. Based on the first sentence, the reader can tell this text is

Ⓐ biographical in nature.
Ⓑ autobiographical in nature.
Ⓒ science fiction.
Ⓓ a scientific text on deserts.

2. What is the purpose for reading this text?

Ⓐ to gain biographical knowledge of an author
Ⓑ to learn about the character of Frankenstein
Ⓒ for entertainment
Ⓓ for entertainment and to learn about Shelley Percy

3. Shelley wrote *Frankenstein* because

Ⓐ she and her friends wanted to see who could write the best ghost story.
Ⓑ she wanted to make her father happy.
Ⓒ she had many dreams and wanted to write about them.
Ⓓ she wanted to make a new kind of creature, but realized she went too far.

4. Mary probably wrote with

Ⓐ a computer.
Ⓑ a typewriter.
Ⓒ a pen.
Ⓓ a piece of chalk.

5. Why did Mary go to school?

Ⓐ because her father thought she should
Ⓑ because it was required
Ⓒ to avoid her stepmother
Ⓓ to meet Percy Shelley

6. Which do you think helped Mary to become a writer?

Ⓐ She and Percy went to Italy.
Ⓑ Her father thought that girls should learn just the same as boys.
Ⓒ Her father married again after four years.
Ⓓ Mary had two children, Clara and William.

SCORE

1. Ⓨ Ⓝ
2. Ⓨ Ⓝ
3. Ⓨ Ⓝ
4. Ⓨ Ⓝ
5. Ⓨ Ⓝ
6. Ⓨ Ⓝ

___ / 6 Total

NAME: ______________________ **DATE:** ______________

SCORE

___ / 4

DIRECTIONS Reread "Mary Shelley." Then, read the prompt and respond on the lines below.

See if you can think of a good ghost story. Explain what your story would be about.

NAME: ______________________ **DATE:** ______________

DIRECTIONS Read the text and then answer the questions.

I couldn't believe it when my sister, Diane, told me she was engaged! "When are you and Pete getting married?" I asked. Pete is Diane's fiancé.

"The wedding will be September 18th," Diane said, "so we'll need to start planning everything."

"But September's almost a year away," I said. "Are weddings that complicated? Do they take that much planning?"

"Absolutely, Angie," said Diane. "We need to reserve a place for the wedding and reception. We need to order the invitations. And then there's the dress, shoes, flowers, and the wedding cake. It's a lot of work."

1. What is **not** involved in planning a wedding?

- (A) reserving a place
- (B) ordering invitations
- (C) talking to friends
- (D) getting a wedding cake

2. The setting of this text is likely

- (A) Diane's wedding reception.
- (B) the middle of a desert.
- (C) the family breakfast table.
- (D) a large warehouse.

3. Which is the suffix in the word *absolutely*?

- (A) *–ly*
- (B) *ab–*
- (C) *–ely*
- (D) *–solute–*

4. A ______ is someone who is about to get married.

- (A) fiancé
- (B) complicated
- (C) wedding
- (D) reserve

5. What type of text would have a similar tone?

- (A) a story about teachers planning a school carnival
- (B) a scientific paper on goose migration in Canada
- (C) a book about a girl who likes to write
- (D) none of the above

SCORE

1. (Y)(N)
2. (Y)(N)
3. (Y)(N)
4. (Y)(N)
5. (Y)(N)

___ / 5
Total

NAME: ______________________________ **DATE:** __________________

DIRECTIONS Read the text and then answer the questions.

SCORE

1. Ⓨ Ⓝ
2. Ⓨ Ⓝ
3. Ⓨ Ⓝ
4. Ⓨ Ⓝ
5. Ⓨ Ⓝ

___ / 5 Total

My sister, Diane, started planning her wedding. I was curious, so I asked who would be in the wedding.

"Pete's friend, Doug, will be his best man, and my best friend, Nan, will be my maid of honor," Diane answered. "There will be bridesmaids and groomsmen, too. They will help to manage all of the little details of the ceremony. That way, the groom and I can concentrate on getting married."

"What about me? Will I be a bridesmaid?" I wanted to be in the wedding.

"You're too young, Angie," Diane said. "But you can be a flower girl."

1. What role will Angie have in Diane's wedding?

Ⓐ maid of honor
Ⓑ bridesmaid
Ⓒ flower girl
Ⓓ bride

2. Which title best fits this text?

Ⓐ A Sister Called Diane
Ⓑ Nan and Doug
Ⓒ Wedding Details
Ⓓ How People Dress at Weddings

3. Which is the root word in *wedding*?

Ⓐ ding
Ⓑ we
Ⓒ wed
Ⓓ edding

4. Someone who is *curious*

Ⓐ wants to eat dinner.
Ⓑ wants to know something.
Ⓒ wants to take a nap.
Ⓓ wants to be alone.

5. What is a *best man*?

Ⓐ the man who helps the groom
Ⓑ a man who is better than everyone
Ⓒ someone who has won a competition
Ⓓ none of the above

NAME:_______________________ DATE:_______________

DIRECTIONS Read the text and then answer the questions.

My sister Diane's wedding was getting closer. She had found the perfect wedding gown. She found very pretty dresses for the bridesmaids, too. I was going to be a flower girl. So my dress didn't look exactly the same as the others. But it was a beautiful blue dress. Diane and her fiancé, Pete, also found the wedding rings they wanted. They were the most beautiful rings I'd ever seen. They were gold with pretty designs.

"Those rings are totally gorgeous!" I told Diane. "They're awfully small, though, aren't they? Don't you and Pete get worried about losing them?"

"We'll be extremely careful with them, so that won't happen," Diane said.

1. Which question best relates to the text?

- (A) Does the flower girl have to wear a blue dress, or can it be yellow?
- (B) Will there be a wedding cake?
- (C) Is the wedding getting closer?
- (D) What kind of items do people purchase before a wedding?

2. Which phrase would make the text fantasy?

- (A) that wrapped around like ivy
- (B) that sparkled brightly
- (C) that turned the wearer invisible
- (D) that was completed when the rings were side by side

3. Which shows the correct pronunciation of *gorgeous*?

- (A) gawr-JUHS
- (B) GAWR-juhs
- (C) GAWR-jee-uhs
- (D) gawr-JEE-uhs

4. Which is a synonym of *totally*?

- (A) ugly
- (B) completely
- (C) partly
- (D) absently

5. In which point of view is the story told?

- (A) first person
- (B) second person
- (C) third person
- (D) There is no point of view.

SCORE

1. (Y)(N)
2. (Y)(N)
3. (Y)(N)
4. (Y)(N)
5. (Y)(N)

___ / 5 Total

NAME: ______________________ **DATE:** ______________

ANGIE SAVES THE WEDDING

It was the morning of my sister, Diane's, wedding. Everyone was rushing around getting ready for the ceremony. When we arrived at the church, I noticed that we were the first ones there.

"Why do we have to get here so early?" I wondered.

"The photographer will take pictures of everyone before the ceremony, so we have to be ready," Mom explained.

Soon the bridesmaids and groomsmen arrived, and the photographer got to work. She took pictures of everyone! Finally, the pictures were finished, and it was almost time to start the ceremony. Suddenly, I heard a voice calling out, "I can't find them anywhere!"

It was Pete, Diane's fiancé. I raced over to Pete to see what was wrong. When I asked him, he said, "I thought I brought the wedding rings with me, Angie. But I just looked in my pocket and I can't find them. Diane is going to be furious!"

"I could help you look for them," I suggested. Pete thanked me and said that would be a big help.

My search began in Pete's car, but I didn't see anything on Pete's driver's seat. My next stop was a little park across the street. The photographer had taken some pictures there. Maybe Pete had dropped the rings there. I looked all over the ground, but I couldn't find them.

Finally I went back inside and found the photographer. I asked her if she had taken any other pictures of Pete.

She answered, "I took pictures of him and the groomsmen near that table."

I went over to the table. There wasn't anything on top of the table, but I had an idea. What if the rings had fallen off the table? I got down on my hands and knees and peered under the table. There they were! I fished them out and brought them to Pete just in time for the ceremony. Pete said, "Angie, you saved the day!"

NAME: ______________________ **DATE:** ______________

DIRECTIONS Read "Angie Saves the Wedding" and then answer the questions.

1. The title indicates that this story is about

Ⓐ something at school.
Ⓑ something that happens at a wedding.
Ⓒ a car trip.
Ⓓ a move to a new city.

2. What is the purpose for reading this text?

Ⓐ for entertainment, to see how a character handles a conflict
Ⓑ for entertainment, to see how a character handles a solution
Ⓒ for information, and specifically to learn about weddings
Ⓓ for information, and specifically to learn about photography

3. Which place doesn't Angie look for the rings?

Ⓐ in Pete's car
Ⓑ in Diane's dressing room
Ⓒ under a table
Ⓓ in a park

4. How does Angie probably feel about finding the rings?

Ⓐ upset
Ⓑ jealous
Ⓒ frightened
Ⓓ proud

5. Is Angie's strategy for finding the missing rings reasonable?

Ⓐ Yes, it was a good strategy because she checked everywhere Pete had been.
Ⓑ Yes, but she didn't need to check under the table or in the car.
Ⓒ No, she is lucky she found them at all.
Ⓓ No, she should have just asked Pete where he put them.

6. In the end, Angie learns

Ⓐ to be aggressive and to work quickly.
Ⓑ that waiting for a problem to fix itself is always best.
Ⓒ that staying calm and thinking through a situation helps.
Ⓓ a lot about wedding rings and how easy they are to lose.

SCORE

1. Ⓨ Ⓝ
2. Ⓨ Ⓝ
3. Ⓨ Ⓝ
4. Ⓨ Ⓝ
5. Ⓨ Ⓝ
6. Ⓨ Ⓝ

___ / 6
Total

NAME: ______________________________ **DATE:** __________________

SCORE

___ / 4

DIRECTIONS Reread "Angie Saves the Wedding." Then, read the prompt and respond on the lines below.

Have you ever been to a wedding? What was it like? If you have never been to a wedding, what kind of wedding would you like to go to? Write about it.

NAME: ______________________ **DATE:** ______________

DIRECTIONS Read the text and then answer the questions.

Some things that you want to have are not too expensive, and you don't need to have a lot of money to get them. But other things cost more, so you need to save up for those things. For example, suppose you want a new computer or bike. You need to save up money for those things because they cost a lot. You could keep your money in a special place in your room, but you might lose it. You might also spend it instead of saving it. Then, you will not be able to buy what you want. That's why many people save their money in a bank account. A bank account is a good way to save your money. You will not lose your money if you put it in the bank. You will not forget to save your money if it is in the bank.

1. Which is a safe place to keep money?

Ⓐ under the bed
Ⓑ in the freezer
Ⓒ in a bank account
Ⓓ on a shelf

2. Which sentence most closely captures the main idea?

Ⓐ For example, suppose you want a new computer or bike.
Ⓑ But other things cost more, so you need to save up for those things.
Ⓒ That's why many people save their money in a bank account.
Ⓓ You will not forget to save your money if it is in the bank.

3. The root word in *expensive* is

Ⓐ ex.
Ⓑ pen.
Ⓒ expend.
Ⓓ expense.

4. The opposite of *forget* is

Ⓐ remember.
Ⓑ save.
Ⓒ buy.
Ⓓ expensive.

5. This text is most like

Ⓐ a biography on money.
Ⓑ a chapter book on investing.
Ⓒ a collection of money-themed poems.
Ⓓ a fable featuring bank tellers.

SCORE

1. Ⓨ Ⓝ
2. Ⓨ Ⓝ
3. Ⓨ Ⓝ
4. Ⓨ Ⓝ
5. Ⓨ Ⓝ

___ / 5
Total

NAME: ______________________ **DATE:** ______________

DIRECTIONS Read the text and then answer the questions.

SCORE

1. Ⓨ Ⓝ

2. Ⓨ Ⓝ

3. Ⓨ Ⓝ

4. Ⓨ Ⓝ

5. Ⓨ Ⓝ

___ / 5
Total

Banks do many different things. One thing banks do is store money securely. When you put your money in a bank account, it is safe. It will be ready for you when you want it. Banks also make loans. Sometimes, people need to buy things that are more expensive than everyday items. For example, suppose your parents want to buy a car; the bank can lend your parents the money. The bank charges your parents money for the loan. That money is called *interest*. Your parents pay the interest back, too. Where does the bank get the money for loans? From people who have their money in bank accounts. The bank uses its customers' money for loans. When people pay their loans, the bank puts the money back in the customers' accounts. The bank pays them to use their money. That is called interest, too.

1. A diagram in which order makes the most sense?

Ⓐ withdraw money from bank, spend money, free money from bank

Ⓑ deposit money in bank, borrow money from bank, bank pays you back extra

Ⓒ deposit money in bank, bank borrows your money, bank pays you back less

Ⓓ deposit money in bank, bank borrows your money, bank pays you back extra

2. Which would help you find the meaning of the word *interest*?

Ⓐ a table of contents

Ⓑ an appendix

Ⓒ the preface

Ⓓ none of the above

3. *Customers'* has

Ⓐ two syllables.

Ⓑ three syllables.

Ⓒ four syllables.

Ⓓ none of the above

4. Which is an antonym of *lend*?

Ⓐ borrow

Ⓑ give

Ⓒ advance

Ⓓ beginning

5. What is the author's purpose?

Ⓐ to inform

Ⓑ to persuade

Ⓒ to instruct

Ⓓ to entertain

NAME: ____________________ **DATE:** ______________

DIRECTIONS Read the text and then answer the questions.

Banks are safe places to keep money, but most people don't want to go to a bank every time they need money. Instead, many people prefer to use debit cards. Here's how a debit card works. Suppose you go shopping and you want to buy a nice shirt. When it's your turn to pay, you slide your debit card through a card reader. The card reader takes money from your bank account. It moves that money to the store's account. You can also get cash with a debit card. To do that, you use an ATM. You insert your debit card into the ATM. It takes money out of your bank account. Then, it gives you the money in cash. ATMs and card readers work very quickly. Everything happens in seconds.

1. Which question could best help a reader understand this text?

- (A) How are people's debit cards connected to their bank accounts?
- (B) How large are debit cards, and are they heavy?
- (C) Where can a person find an ATM?
- (D) What percent of people prefer using debit cards?

2. Which index entry would help a reader locate the text?

- (A) credit-card tips
- (B) shopping for clothes
- (C) things that happen quickly
- (D) credit and debit card usage

3. Which word does **not** have a suffix?

- (A) debit
- (B) quickly
- (C) works
- (D) happens

4. Another way to say *prefer to* is

- (A) do not know how to.
- (B) are afraid to.
- (C) would rather.
- (D) do not like to.

5. This text is most like

- (A) an autobiographical text on the president.
- (B) a theater program.
- (C) an expository text on using computers.
- (D) a fantasy novel about vampires.

SCORE

1. Ⓨ Ⓝ

2. Ⓨ Ⓝ

3. Ⓨ Ⓝ

4. Ⓨ Ⓝ

5. Ⓨ Ⓝ

___ / 5

Total

NAME: ______________________ **DATE:** ______________

BANK ON IT!

Banks are very important in our lives. Why? How did they get to be so important? Long ago, people had to trade things to get what they wanted; now, people use money. But it isn't a good idea to keep a lot of money in your home. For one thing, you might lose it. And if you dropped your money somewhere, someone might take it. That's why most people keep their money in banks.

There are many kinds of bank accounts, but most people have savings accounts and checking accounts. People use savings accounts to save up for big things. You might use a savings account to save up for college, a vacation, or a car. People use checking accounts to pay bills and buy food and other things they need.

Banks do not just keep people's money in one place, though. They use that money to make loans for people. People get loans when they need something expensive. You might get a loan to buy a car. Banks charge interest on those loans. When people pay back their loans, they also pay the interest. That's how banks make their money.

Do you have a bank account? If you do, then you make money, too! How does that happen? The bank uses your money to make loans. It also uses money that other people put in the bank. The bank pays you interest to use your money. Is your money always there when you want it? Yes! Many people keep their money in the bank. And people pay their loans back. So the bank always has plenty of money. When you are ready to get your money, it is ready for you. The more money you keep in the bank, the more interest you will earn.

Banks have changed a lot over the years. Today, many people use debit cards instead of cash. They also use online banking. Now, people can use the bank any time they want.

NAME:______________________ DATE:______________

DIRECTIONS Read "Bank On It!" and then answer the questions.

1. After reading this text, a reader will know

Ⓐ more about banks.
Ⓑ more about bank accounts.
Ⓒ more about loans and when to use them.
Ⓓ all of the above

2. The author most likely wrote this

Ⓐ to tell about history.
Ⓑ to tell a personal story.
Ⓒ to get you to buy something.
Ⓓ to tell how banks work.

3. How do banks make their money?

Ⓐ Many people use online banking.
Ⓑ They give you interest.
Ⓒ They charge interest when they make loans.
Ⓓ Many people use debit cards.

4. The author proposes that people keep their money in a bank to

Ⓐ keep it safe and to pay interest on their money.
Ⓑ keep it safe and to earn interest on their money.
Ⓒ help out banks so they don't go out of business.
Ⓓ keep it safe, but that they should also keep a piggy bank.

5. Why might you put money into a savings account?

Ⓐ for a vacation
Ⓑ for the phone bill
Ⓒ for food
Ⓓ for a pair of socks

6. What is the main idea?

Ⓐ People get loans when they need a car.
Ⓑ Never take your money out of the bank.
Ⓒ Banks help people with savings and loans.
Ⓓ It's better to trade than use money.

SCORE

1. Ⓨ Ⓝ
2. Ⓨ Ⓝ
3. Ⓨ Ⓝ
4. Ⓨ Ⓝ
5. Ⓨ Ⓝ
6. Ⓨ Ⓝ

___ / 6 Total

NAME: ______________________________ **DATE:** ________________

DIRECTIONS Reread "Bank On It!" Then, read the prompt and respond on the lines below.

SCORE

___ / 4

Do you have a bank account? Are you saving up for something special? Write about what you are saving for or what you would like to save for.

NAME: ______________________ **DATE:** ______________

DIRECTIONS Read the text and then answer the questions.

Alex walked to school every morning. He passed several stores on his way to school, but one of the more interesting shops was a video game store called GameBegin. Alex loved video games, so he sometimes stopped into the store. One day, he noticed a new game called *Time Travel*. Alex was excited—the game looked like so much fun! He decided he wanted the game. But it was expensive, and Alex knew his parents would not buy such an expensive game for him. He would have to save his money. But it would take time to save up the money, and Alex was afraid the store would not have the game once he was ready to buy it. Then, Alex had an idea. "My birthday's coming up next month," he thought. "I'll ask for the game as a birthday present, and then Mom and Dad will get it for me."

1. Which game does Alex decide to buy?
   - Ⓐ GameBegin
   - Ⓑ Expensive Game
   - Ⓒ Time Travel
   - Ⓓ all of the above

2. The dialogue in the text shows that Alex is
   - Ⓐ careful.
   - Ⓑ hopeful.
   - Ⓒ cunning.
   - Ⓓ sophisticated.

3. How is the word *expensive* pronounced?
   - Ⓐ x-SPEN-siv
   - Ⓑ ik-SPEN-siv
   - Ⓒ ik-SPENS-iv
   - Ⓓ ikspens-IV

4. *Several* means
   - Ⓐ a few.
   - Ⓑ one.
   - Ⓒ many.
   - Ⓓ more than a few.

5. In this text, *coming up* means
   - Ⓐ far away.
   - Ⓑ visiting.
   - Ⓒ rising.
   - Ⓓ about to happen.

SCORE

1. Ⓨ Ⓝ
2. Ⓨ Ⓝ
3. Ⓨ Ⓝ
4. Ⓨ Ⓝ
5. Ⓨ Ⓝ

___ / 5 Total

NAME: ______________________ **DATE:** ______________

DIRECTIONS Read the text and then answer the questions.

SCORE

1. Ⓨ Ⓝ
2. Ⓨ Ⓝ
3. Ⓨ Ⓝ
4. Ⓨ Ⓝ
5. Ⓨ Ⓝ

___ / 5 Total

Alex and his friends sat at the dining room table. The table was covered with a pile of presents. Alex knew exactly which present he wanted to open first. He pulled it from the pile and tore open the wrapping paper.

"I knew it!" he shouted triumphantly. The present was a video game called *Time Travel* that Alex had been wanting for a month. He'd been hopeful that his parents would give it to him. He thanked his parents and then passed the game around so his friends could see it, too.

"This is amazing," said Alex's friend Corey. "I've wanted this game since it came out. You're incredibly lucky."

"Now that I have it," Alex said, "you can come over and we can both play it."

1. Which suggests the text takes place at a birthday party?

Ⓐ *The table was covered with a pile of presents.*

Ⓑ *"I knew it!" he shouted triumphantly.*

Ⓒ *Alex and his friends sat at his dining room table.*

Ⓓ *"Now that I have it," Alex said, "you can come over and we can both play it."*

2. This story takes place

Ⓐ at breakfast.

Ⓑ at school.

Ⓒ at a birthday party.

Ⓓ at a video game store.

3. The root word in *wrapping* is

Ⓐ rap.

Ⓑ wrapp.

Ⓒ ping.

Ⓓ wrap.

4. Which is a synonym for *triumphantly*?

Ⓐ seriously

Ⓑ with difficultly

Ⓒ victoriously

Ⓓ happily

5. *Tore open* tells you that Alex is

Ⓐ bored with the present.

Ⓑ in a hurry to see the present.

Ⓒ afraid to see the present.

Ⓓ not interested in the present.

NAME: ______________________ **DATE:** ______________

DIRECTIONS Read the text and then answer the questions.

Alex and his friend, Corey, were playing Alex's new video game called *Time Travel*. Alex's little sister, Pam, came in the room and asked, "What are you guys doing? Can I play, too? I don't have anything to do."

"We're playing *Time Travel*," Alex mumbled. He didn't want to have a conversation with Pam. And he didn't want Pam to play the game.

"What's *Time Travel* about?" she asked. "How do you play the game?"

Alex answered briefly, "You have to survive during ancient times. If you're not careful, the dinosaurs attack and then you lose."

"Forget it," Pam said. "That sounds really boring. I'd rather play soccer."

Alex and Corey could not believe anyone would think *Time Travel* was boring!

1. Why does Pam decide that she doesn't want to play with Alex and Corey?

- Ⓐ because they are playing a boring game
- Ⓑ because she doesn't like Corey
- Ⓒ because she doesn't know how to time-travel
- Ⓓ because she likes soccer

2. Which is the most likely setting?

- Ⓐ in Alex's parents' living room
- Ⓑ in an arcade
- Ⓒ at school
- Ⓓ at the public library

3. *Mumbled* is pronounced

- Ⓐ MUHM-buhld
- Ⓑ muhm-BUHLD
- Ⓒ MUHM-buhl-ed
- Ⓓ muhm-BUHL-ed

4. The root word in *briefly* is

- Ⓐ fly.
- Ⓑ brie.
- Ⓒ brief.
- Ⓓ rief.

5. The word *mumbled* tells you that Alex is

- Ⓐ yelling.
- Ⓑ laughing.
- Ⓒ speaking clearly.
- Ⓓ speaking quietly.

SCORE

1. Ⓨ Ⓝ
2. Ⓨ Ⓝ
3. Ⓨ Ⓝ
4. Ⓨ Ⓝ
5. Ⓨ Ⓝ

___ / 5
Total

NAME: ______________________________ **DATE:** ________________

IT'S JUST ONE GAME...

One day, Alex and his friend, Corey, decided to visit Games and More, a video-game store near their school. They looked around the store and found all sorts of new games.

"These games are so awesome," Alex said. "I wish I could have every one of them."

"I know," Corey answered. "The one I want most is *Time Travel*. I really love playing it."

"It's an amazing game," Alex agreed. "And I hear they're coming out with another version."

For a while, the two boys looked through the selection of games. Then, Alex noticed that the store had a new game system on display. He wandered over to look at it. While Alex was looking at the game system, Corey was still looking at the games. He saw a few copies of *Time Travel* right there in front of him. Nobody would notice if he took just one.

Alex turned around and saw Corey pick up a copy of the game and slip it in his jacket. He rushed back to his friend. "What are you doing?" he hissed angrily.

"Shhh!" Corey insisted. "Nobody will notice anything."

"You can't just take that game! That's stealing, and you'll get in serious trouble."

"Alex, come on," Corey insisted. "It's only one game. Nobody will notice anything. Besides, I could never afford it myself."

"Forget it, Corey," Alex snapped. "I'm not letting you steal. Now, put it back or I'm calling the manager."

"Are you seriously going to do that?" Corey asked.

"Of course I'm going to do it. Put the game back!"

The two boys glared at each other for what seemed like hours. Finally, Corey put his hand in his pocket, drew the game back out, and placed it back in the slot where it belonged. Then, he said, "I'm really sorry. I almost made a huge mistake."

"Yeah, you almost did. But it is an amazing game. I'll let you borrow it."

NAME: ____________________ **DATE:** ____________

DIRECTIONS Read "It's Just One Game…" and then answer the questions.

1. After reading this text, a reader will be better able to

(A) steal video games.
(B) consider right and wrong.
(C) hide things from their friends.
(D) argue about why stealing is sometimes okay.

2. The author probably wrote this to

(A) show an audience a nice way to resolve a *what's right and what's wrong* conflict.
(B) show an audience how to control and ignore your friends.
(C) show an audience how to argue and always be right.
(D) entertain an audience with a fun story before recess.

3. What do you predict will happen next?

(A) Alex will take a video game.
(B) Corey will not be friends with Alex.
(C) Alex will tell the manager what Corey did.
(D) Alex and Corey will play *Time Travel* at Alex's house.

4. The conflict in this text is between

(A) Alex and himself.
(B) Corey and the store manager.
(C) Alex and the store manager.
(D) Alex and Corey.

5. Why do you think Alex stops Corey from taking the game?

(A) He doesn't see Corey take the game.
(B) He wants the game for himself.
(C) He doesn't want his best friend to be a thief.
(D) He doesn't want to take the game.

6. This text is an example of a(n) ______ situation.

(A) ethical
(B) video-game store
(C) fun
(D) miraculous

SCORE

1. (Y)(N)
2. (Y)(N)
3. (Y)(N)
4. (Y)(N)
5. (Y)(N)
6. (Y)(N)

___ / 6
Total

NAME: ______________________________ **DATE:** ________________

SCORE

___ / 4

DIRECTIONS

Reread "It's Just One Game...." Then, read the prompt and respond on the lines below.

What would you do if you were in Alex's situation? Explain what you would do.

NAME: ____________________ **DATE:** ______________

DIRECTIONS Read the text and then answer the questions.

What color are your hair and your eyes? What about your skin? How tall are you? Your eye color, hair color, skin color, and height are all attributes of your appearance, or the way you look. Now, think about your friends' appearances. They look different from you. Perhaps their eyes, hair, or skin is a different color from yours. How does that happen, and why do you look the way you look? The answer is because of genes (jeenz), which determine your appearance. Thousands of genes are in each cell of your body. But despite their size, genes are very important. Genes tell your body what color your eyes, hair, and skin will be. They determine your height and explain why everyone looks different. Everyone has his or her own unique set of genes.

1. What determines the color of a person's eyes?

- (A) skin color
- (B) genes
- (C) a grandparent
- (D) where a person was born

2. Which summarizes the text?

- (A) Everyone looks different because of their eye color.
- (B) Genes control our appearance, but they don't really matter.
- (C) Genes control our appearance, and everyone has his or her own unique set of genes.
- (D) Genes are very small; even an ant is larger.

3. Which of the following is a homophone of *genes*?

- (A) spleens
- (B) generous
- (C) genius
- (D) jeans

4. Based on the context of the text, *determine* means

- (A) to dislike.
- (B) to discuss and decide.
- (C) to like how something will be.
- (D) to control the limits of.

5. What is the author's purpose?

- (A) to entertain
- (B) to inform
- (C) to persuade
- (D) to instruct

SCORE

1. Ⓨ Ⓝ
2. Ⓨ Ⓝ
3. Ⓨ Ⓝ
4. Ⓨ Ⓝ
5. Ⓨ Ⓝ

___ / 5
Total

NAME: ______________________ **DATE:** ______________

DIRECTIONS Read the text and then answer the questions.

SCORE

1. Ⓨ Ⓝ

2. Ⓨ Ⓝ

3. Ⓨ Ⓝ

4. Ⓨ Ⓝ

5. Ⓨ Ⓝ

___ / 5

Total

Although genes are extremely small, they have a lot of work to do. In fact, you have thousands of genes. Each gene has its own special job. For example, think about your eyes—are they brown, blue, green, a mixture, or some other color? Maybe they are gray, or maybe they change color with your moods. You have a special gene that controls what color your eyes will be. Another gene controls the color of your skin. You may have light skin or very dark skin. Regardless of your skin color, there is a unique gene that tells your body what color your skin will be. Your genes even tell your body whether you will have freckles! There is a special gene in charge of your height, too. It tells your body how tall you will be when you grow up. Your genes work together to make you look the way you look.

1. Which is not determined by a person's genes?

Ⓐ eye color

Ⓑ T-shirt color

Ⓒ skin color

Ⓓ hair color

2. Which title best fits this text?

Ⓐ Telling My Body

Ⓑ Height

Ⓒ I Am Tall

Ⓓ Your Genes and You

3. Which word does not have a long *e* vowel sound?

Ⓐ unique

Ⓑ gene

Ⓒ example

Ⓓ maybe

4. Which is another way to say *how tall you are*?

Ⓐ height

Ⓑ genes

Ⓒ eye color

Ⓓ freckles

5. Which word is possessive?

Ⓐ each

Ⓑ job

Ⓒ its

Ⓓ gene

NAME: ____________________ **DATE:** ____________

DIRECTIONS Read the text and then answer the questions.

Where do your genes come from, and how do you get them? You get your genes from your parents. Think about your mom's and dad's physical characteristics. Both of your parents have thousands of genes. Your parents passed copies of their genes to you when you were born. Half your genes come from your mother, and the other half come from your father. For example, each parent gives you a gene for eye color. If both parents give you a gene for brown eyes, then you will have brown eyes, too. But imagine your mother gave you a gene for blue eyes and your father gave you a gene for brown eyes. The gene for brown eyes is the dominant gene, so your eyes will be brown. Still, you received one eye-color gene from each parent.

1. Where do a person's genes come from?

Ⓐ all from the mother
Ⓑ half from each parent
Ⓒ all from the father
Ⓓ half from two grandparents

2. Which index entry would help a reader locate the text?

Ⓐ brown eyes
Ⓑ characters in time
Ⓒ your parents
Ⓓ genes mixing together

3. Which is the stressed syllable in the word *dominant*?

Ⓐ the first syllable
Ⓑ the second syllable
Ⓒ the third syllable
Ⓓ none of the above

4. Which is the antonym of *both*?

Ⓐ some
Ⓑ neither
Ⓒ one
Ⓓ each

5. The term *physical characteristics* means

Ⓐ how a person looks.
Ⓑ what a person thinks.
Ⓒ the character of a person.
Ⓓ physical items that have character.

SCORE

1. Ⓨ Ⓝ
2. Ⓨ Ⓝ
3. Ⓨ Ⓝ
4. Ⓨ Ⓝ
5. Ⓨ Ⓝ

___ / 5
Total

NAME: ____________________ DATE: ______________

IT'S ALL IN THE GENES

What do you have in common with a pumpkin, a panda, and a basset hound? The answer is genes. Every living thing has genes. The set of genes for each living thing is different. That is why you do not look the same as your friends. It is also why you do not look like a pumpkin, a panda, or a basset hound. Your genes are unique to you. They are in charge of your eye color, your hair color, and your height. They are part of what makes you the person you are.

Pumpkins have genes, too. Pumpkin genes are in charge of the pumpkin's shape and color. They are in charge of the shape of its leaves. There are genes in every pumpkin seed. They tell the seed that it will become a pumpkin. If you plant a pumpkin seed, it will grow into a pumpkin, not an oak tree. That is because the seed has pumpkin genes in it.

What about pandas? Pandas have genes, too. Those genes tell the panda's body that it will have black and white fur. They also tell the panda's body that it will have black ears and black circles around its eyes. Mother pandas and father pandas have black ears and black circles around their eyes. They have black-and-white fur. They pass those genes to their babies, just as your parents passed their genes to you.

Have you ever seen a basset hound? Basset hounds have long, droopy ears, long bodies, and short legs. They also have an excellent sense of smell. How does a basset hound get those floppy ears, long bodies, and sense of smell? The genes in charge of its body shape make its body long and low to the ground. The basset hound's keen sense of smell comes from genes, too. The basset hound is only one breed of dog with its own special genes. Other breeds of dog have different genes. That is why basset hounds do not look like golden retrievers. Each living thing has its own special genes.

NAME: ______________________ **DATE:** ______________

DIRECTIONS Read "It's All in the Genes" and then answer the questions.

SCORE

1. A reader can predict that basset hounds will have

Ⓐ puppies with very long legs.

Ⓑ puppies that do not have floppy ears.

Ⓒ puppies that do not have a good sense of smell.

Ⓓ puppies that look like their parents.

2. What is the author's purpose?

Ⓐ to tell how genes make living things different

Ⓑ to get you to adopt a basset hound

Ⓒ to tell how pumpkins grow

Ⓓ to tell you where you can go to see pandas

3. Which statement is true?

Ⓐ Only some living things have genes.

Ⓑ All dogs have the same genes.

Ⓒ Each living thing has unique genes.

Ⓓ Children have the same genes as their parents.

4. Where do genes come from?

Ⓐ parents

Ⓑ pumpkins

Ⓒ pandas

Ⓓ basset hounds

5. Which does **not** have genes?

Ⓐ water

Ⓑ dogs

Ⓒ whales

Ⓓ ladybugs

6. Which is a good summary of this text?

Ⓐ Pumpkins and pandas do not look the same.

Ⓑ All living things have genes, and each has its own special genes.

Ⓒ Panda mothers and fathers pass their genes to their babies.

Ⓓ Your genes determine your hair color, eye color, and height.

1. Ⓨ Ⓝ

2. Ⓨ Ⓝ

3. Ⓨ Ⓝ

4. Ⓨ Ⓝ

5. Ⓨ Ⓝ

6. Ⓨ Ⓝ

___ / 6

Total

NAME: ______________________ **DATE:** ______________

DIRECTIONS Reread "It's All in the Genes." Then, read the prompt and respond on the lines below.

SCORE

___ / 4

Where did you get your eye color? Your hair color? Your skin color? Your height? Do you look more like your father? More like your mother? Write about how your genes determine the way you look.

NAME: ______________________ **DATE:** ________________

DIRECTIONS Read the text and then answer the questions.

It was a beautiful autumn afternoon. Tricia decided to go home from school by taking a new route (ROOT). Usually, she walked home using the most direct route—three blocks south and eight blocks west. But today, it was just too beautiful to go straight home. This time, she went two blocks north, and then eight blocks west. Tricia was about to turn south to go to her house when she saw a creek with a small stream of water running through it on the left side of the road. Tricia crossed the street and went to the bank of the creek. She looked up and down the bank, but she didn't see anyone nearby. Tricia thought, "I never even knew there was a creek here. It's hard to believe there's a creek in the middle of the city."

1. The first sentence suggests

- (A) this will be a fictional text.
- (B) this will be an expository text.
- (C) this will be a scientific text.
- (D) this will be a biography.

2. Tricia learns that on the different route home,

- (A) there are more trees.
- (B) there is a pond.
- (C) there is a creek.
- (D) there are less trees.

3. Which word has the same vowel sound as *through*?

- (A) blocks
- (B) too
- (C) looked
- (D) thought

4. Which is a synonym for *route*?

- (A) way
- (B) creek
- (C) street
- (D) block

5. What does the *most direct route* mean?

- (A) the longest way
- (B) the straightest way
- (C) the prettiest way
- (D) the cheapest way

SCORE

1. Ⓨ Ⓝ

2. Ⓨ Ⓝ

3. Ⓨ Ⓝ

4. Ⓨ Ⓝ

5. Ⓨ Ⓝ

___ / 5 Total

NAME: ______________________ **DATE:** ______________

DIRECTIONS Read the text and then answer the questions.

SCORE

1. Ⓨ Ⓝ
2. Ⓨ Ⓝ
3. Ⓨ Ⓝ
4. Ⓨ Ⓝ
5. Ⓨ Ⓝ

___ / 5 **Total**

Tricia had just found a creek a short distance from her house. She liked sitting on the bank of the creek. The green moss Tricia used as a seat was as soft as velvet and very comfortable. From her velvet seat, Tricia could observe the creek. She could see the trees on the creek banks as they swayed gently in the breeze. They were losing their orange, red, and yellow leaves. Tricia liked watching the creek water and hearing it rush softly by. Sometimes, she saw frogs there. Once, she saw a salamander. She saw turtles, too, and a lot of insects. The creek sounded alive with noise. She heard croaking frogs. She also heard buzzing insects. Sometimes, Tricia wished she could live at the creek.

1. Which title would most appropriately fit this text?

Ⓐ Bank
Ⓑ And Turtles Too
Ⓒ Sitting Down on Something Soft
Ⓓ At the Creek

2. The setting of the text is a creek, but it could also take place at

Ⓐ a beach.
Ⓑ a pond.
Ⓒ a school.
Ⓓ a factory.

3. Which shows the correct pronunciation of *salamander*?

Ⓐ sal-UH-man-der
Ⓑ SAL-uh-man-der
Ⓒ sal-uh-MAN-der
Ⓓ sal-uh-man-DER

4. Which is a synonym for *swayed*?

Ⓐ stayed
Ⓑ swung
Ⓒ stood
Ⓓ grew

5. Which of these is a simile?

Ⓐ alive with noise
Ⓑ as soft as velvet
Ⓒ croaking frogs
Ⓓ at the creek

NAME: ______________________ **DATE:** ______________

DIRECTIONS Read the text and then answer the questions.

Tricia decided to invite her friend, Lisa, to see the creek she had found. So one Saturday morning, the two girls headed there. Tricia wasn't sure Lisa would like the creek, but when they got there, Lisa said, "This is beautiful! You are so lucky you found this place!"

Tricia certainly felt lucky. When she was at the creek, she could watch the water and the animals and listen to the sounds they made. She could even bring a book and read. The creek was very peaceful. Lisa thought it was wonderful, too. She said, "We should have a picnic here. We could bring our lunch and spend the whole afternoon. What do you think?"

"Awesome idea!" Tricia answered. "Let's plan to come here next weekend."

1. The first sentence suggests the text is about

- (A) two friends visiting a pond and the fun things they do there.
- (B) two friends visiting a creek and the activities they do there.
- (C) two friends visiting a house and having a picnic there.
- (D) two friends visiting a creek and playing on the rope swing there.

2. How does Lisa feel when Tricia takes her to the creek?

- (A) bored
- (B) confused
- (C) disappointed
- (D) happy

3. Which words have the same suffix?

- (A) *lucky* and *Saturday*
- (B) *peaceful* and *wonderful*
- (C) *certainly* and *beautiful*
- (D) none of the above

4. An antonym of *awesome* is

- (A) stupendous.
- (B) normal.
- (C) radical.
- (D) inspiring.

5. In the text, *whole* refers to

- (A) a nice time.
- (B) an entire length of time.
- (C) a complete sandwich.
- (D) the start of the afternoon.

SCORE

1. (Y) (N)
2. (Y) (N)
3. (Y) (N)
4. (Y) (N)
5. (Y) (N)

___ / 5 Total

NAME:______________________________ DATE:__________________

A VERY WET PICNIC

One Saturday, Tricia and her friend, Lisa, went to their favorite place. It was a creek that Tricia had found. Both girls had a backpack full of supplies. They had planned a picnic, and they had each brought food. Apart from food, Tricia brought a camera and a large bottle of water. Lisa brought water, a pad of paper, and some pens.

The girls arrived at the creek. Tricia pulled a soft, blue blanket out of her backpack and then took out some sandwiches and two green apples. Lisa opened her backpack and retrieved a banana and a few cookies. For a while, the two girls ate and drank without conversing much. When they finished, Tricia said, "Let's take some pictures." Lisa agreed, and they walked up and down the creek while keeping their eyes out for interesting things. They took pictures of what they saw. They took pictures of frogs and turtles. They took a picture of a salamander, the colorful leaves, and the countless flowers that surrounded them.

Then, Tricia and Lisa decided to draw their surroundings. They drew pictures of what they saw. They drew trees and rocks. They drew the water. They drew some of the animals, too. All of a sudden, Lisa saw a drop fall on her paper. Then, she saw another drop. Then, another fell.

"It's starting to rain, Tricia," Lisa said in a panicked voice. "We need to go, or we'll be soaked."

"Okay, let's pack up," Tricia answered. The two girls quickly put everything in their backpacks. Now the rain was coming down harder. They were going to have to hurry home. They shrugged their backpacks on and sprinted as fast as they could back to Tricia's house. By that time, the storm had worsened. Rain lashed at the windows and thunder boomed. When they got to Tricia's house, they raced inside, dripping water as they went.

"What happened to you two?" asked Tricia's mother.

"We got caught in the rainstorm," Tricia gasped.

Tricia's mother got the two girls some dry towels and helped them with their backpacks. Lisa and Tricia looked at each other and laughed.

"At least we took pictures of our picnic before the rain really started to pour!" Lisa said thankfully.

NAME: ______________________ **DATE:** ______________

DIRECTIONS Read "A Very Wet Picnic" and then answer the questions.

1. What happens as the girls are drawing?

Ⓐ It starts to rain.
Ⓑ Lisa's drink spills.
Ⓒ A salamander approaches them.
Ⓓ They decide to take pictures.

2. The purpose of this text is

Ⓐ to read about rain and wet grass.
Ⓑ to read about what a picnic is.
Ⓒ to read a story from the perspective of one character.
Ⓓ to read a story from the perspective of two different characters.

3. What might happen next?

Ⓐ Lisa and Tricia will go to the creek.
Ⓑ Lisa and Tricia will dry off with the towels.
Ⓒ Lisa and Tricia will eat lunch.
Ⓓ Lisa and Tricia will draw a tree.

4. Why do you think Tricia and Lisa ran as fast as they could?

Ⓐ They are late for dinner.
Ⓑ They are afraid of the dark.
Ⓒ They saw something very scary at the creek.
Ⓓ It is raining very hard, and they want to stay dry.

5. Tricia and Lisa resolve the rain issue by

Ⓐ packing up their picnic to keep things dry.
Ⓑ sprinting to Tricia's house.
Ⓒ taking shelter inside and avoiding the rain.
Ⓓ all of the above

6. This story is an example of

Ⓐ characters goofing around without planning anything out.
Ⓑ characters making plans and keeping them without any changes.
Ⓒ characters making plans but having to change them.
Ⓓ none of the above

SCORE

1. Ⓨ Ⓝ
2. Ⓨ Ⓝ
3. Ⓨ Ⓝ
4. Ⓨ Ⓝ
5. Ⓨ Ⓝ
6. Ⓨ Ⓝ

___ / 6
Total

NAME: ______________________ **DATE:** ______________

DIRECTIONS Reread "A Very Wet Picnic." Then, read the prompt and respond on the lines below.

SCORE

___ / 4

What would you bring with you on a picnic at a creek? What would you want to do there? Write about what you would do.

NAME: ______________________ **DATE:** ______________

DIRECTIONS Read the text and then answer the questions.

Air is constantly moving. Sometimes, air moves north from the Gulf of Mexico. That air is warm and moist because the Gulf of Mexico is warm and moist. Sometimes, air moves south from Canada. That air is cool and dry because it comes from a cool, dry place. Sometimes, a mass of warm, moist air meets a mass of cool, dry air. When that happens, the air masses become unstable. That means they change quickly. Strong winds can begin to blow. If the winds blow fast enough and change direction, they begin to spin, just as water does when it goes down a drain. If a spinning storm doesn't touch the ground, it is called a *funnel*. But if the funnel touches the ground, it is called a *tornado*. Tornados are common in areas where masses of warm and cool air meet.

1. Which question might a reader ask after reading this text?

- (A) Where does cool air come from?
- (B) Does the Gulf of Mexico try to keep its warm air?
- (C) Why can't warm and cool air mix and still be stable?
- (D) all of the above

2. Which of the following would best accompany this text?

- (A) a video showing a tornado forming
- (B) a video of the damage a tornado can cause
- (C) a video of cool air being measured by scientists
- (D) a video of the Gulf of Mexico in the summer

3. Which is the stressed syllable in the word *tornado*?

- (A) the first syllable
- (B) the second syllable
- (C) the third syllable
- (D) none of the above

4. Which is the antonym of *moist*?

- (A) dry
- (B) cold
- (C) hot
- (D) spinning

5. What is the tone of the text?

- (A) formal
- (B) informal
- (C) scary
- (D) silly

SCORE

1. Ⓨ Ⓝ
2. Ⓨ Ⓝ
3. Ⓨ Ⓝ
4. Ⓨ Ⓝ
5. Ⓨ Ⓝ

___ / 5 Total

NAME: ______________________ DATE: ______________

DIRECTIONS Read the text and then answer the questions.

SCORE

1. Ⓨ Ⓝ

2. Ⓨ Ⓝ

3. Ⓨ Ⓝ

4. Ⓨ Ⓝ

5. Ⓨ Ⓝ

___ / 5
Total

Why are tornadoes dangerous? There are two big reasons. One reason is the tornado's winds. The strong winds that form tornadoes move upward. As they spin, they carry things along with them. Some tornadoes are weak. Their winds carry leaves, branches, and dust with them. Other tornadoes are stronger. The winds from strong tornadoes can break windows. They can pull up trees. Very strong tornadoes can knock over buildings and lift cars. The bigger and stronger a tornado is, the more damage it will cause. It is also very hard to tell exactly where a tornado will strike and which direction a tornado will take. So it is hard to warn people when a tornado comes.

1. Which question might a reader ask after reading?

Ⓐ Do large tornadoes cause more damage than small tornadoes?
Ⓑ How fast do tornadoes move?
Ⓒ Can scientists tell which direction a tornado is moving?
Ⓓ Do tornadoes pull up trees?

2. What is something a tornado **cannot** do?

Ⓐ cause an earthquake
Ⓑ break windows
Ⓒ lift cars
Ⓓ knock over buildings

3. Which word is **not** plural?

Ⓐ tornado's
Ⓑ branches
Ⓒ leaves
Ⓓ reasons

4. Another word for *damage* is

Ⓐ building.
Ⓑ reward.
Ⓒ harm.
Ⓓ anger.

5. What is the author's purpose?

Ⓐ to instruct
Ⓑ to entertain
Ⓒ to persuade
Ⓓ to inform

NAME: ____________________ **DATE:** ____________

DIRECTIONS Read the text and then answer the questions.

Tornadoes can be very dangerous. But there are things you can do to be safe. A tornado warning means that a tornado has touched ground. You need to take shelter right away. Here is what to do if you hear a tornado warning:

- Go to a basement. You can also go to an inside room such as a bathroom or closet.
- If you can, get under a sturdy piece of furniture, such as a table.
- If you live in a mobile home, get out.
- If you are in a car, get out.
- If you're outside, go to a ditch or low-lying area and lie flat in it.
- Stay away from fallen power lines and damaged areas.

1. What does a tornado warning mean?

Ⓐ a tornado has touched ground
Ⓑ a tornado may be nearby
Ⓒ people should take shelter
Ⓓ all of the above

2. Which is **not** a good place to take shelter from a tornado?

Ⓐ in a car
Ⓑ in a basement
Ⓒ under a sturdy table
Ⓓ in a closet

3. The root word in *sturdy* is

Ⓐ sturd.
Ⓑ stu.
Ⓒ rude.
Ⓓ none of the above

4. An antonym of *dangerous* is

Ⓐ risky.
Ⓑ deadly.
Ⓒ secure.
Ⓓ none of the above

5. When you *take shelter*, you

Ⓐ run outside.
Ⓑ go to a safe place.
Ⓒ steal someone's shelter.
Ⓓ look for shells.

SCORE

1. Ⓨ Ⓝ
2. Ⓨ Ⓝ
3. Ⓨ Ⓝ
4. Ⓨ Ⓝ
5. Ⓨ Ⓝ

___ / 5
Total

NAME: ____________________ **DATE:** ______________

STORM CHASERS

Some people track, or follow, big storms such as tornadoes. These people are often called *storm chasers*. Their goal is to get as close as they can to storms so that they can observe and record them. They find out where storms such as tornadoes are. Then, they travel to those places to watch the storms. They take pictures and record videos of them. Some storm chasers follow tornadoes. They use equipment to learn about the tornado they are chasing. The equipment shows how fast the tornado is moving and where it is going. It also shows how fast the winds are blowing.

What kind of people become storm chasers? Some storm chasers are scientists. They want to study tornadoes. Other storm chasers track storms because it is their hobby. They find storms very interesting and want to know more about them. A few storm chasers are paid to chase storms. They sell their videos and pictures. They may even offer storm-chasing tours! But most storm chasers are not paid. They chase storms because they are interested in them.

What is it like to chase a storm? Storm chasers travel many, many miles looking for storms. They spend a lot of time in their cars or trucks. They have to be good at using cameras and computers. They also have to be good at recording data. Storm chasers start by checking their computers. They find out where a tornado might hit. Then, they travel to that place. On the way, they check their computers again. Finally, they get to a place where a tornado might strike. When they do, they stop. They set up their equipment. They also look at the sky to see if a tornado will form. If a tornado does form, they observe, take pictures, and then get out of the way. If there is no tornado, they move on to another place. It is not easy to be a storm chaser, but it can be exciting!

NAME:_________________________ DATE:_______________

DIRECTIONS Read “Storm Chasers” and then answer the questions.

1. After having read this text, a reader might

Ⓐ decide to stay inside forever so as to avoid storms.

Ⓑ become more interested in the science of volcanoes.

Ⓒ decide to study the science of animals and living things.

Ⓓ none of the above

2. The author wants the reader to

Ⓐ learn about storm chasers.

Ⓑ take a storm-chasing tour.

Ⓒ learn about computers.

Ⓓ drive a car or truck.

3. Based on the text, which items does a storm chaser need?

Ⓐ rain jacket, computer with GPS tracking, a truck with rain tires

Ⓑ rain jacket, a rubber duck, a computer with GPS tracking

Ⓒ a rubber duck, a truck with rain tires, a car with rain tires

Ⓓ a truck with rain tires, a cotton sweater, a public telephone

4. What do storm chasers do first?

Ⓐ They take pictures and observe.

Ⓑ They travel to a place where a storm might be.

Ⓒ They check their computers to see where a storm might be.

Ⓓ They get out of the way of a storm.

5. Which do storm chasers probably like?

Ⓐ science

Ⓑ history

Ⓒ tennis

Ⓓ music

6. What is storm chasing like?

Ⓐ Storm chasing is quick and easy for most storm chasers. It is also exciting.

Ⓑ Storm chasing can be done at home. That is why it is exciting.

Ⓒ Storm chasing is mostly done by people who are paid to chase storms.

Ⓓ Storm chasing takes a lot of travel and is not easy, but it can be exciting.

SCORE

1. Ⓨ Ⓝ

2. Ⓨ Ⓝ

3. Ⓨ Ⓝ

4. Ⓨ Ⓝ

5. Ⓨ Ⓝ

6. Ⓨ Ⓝ

___ / 6

Total

NAME: ______________________ **DATE:** ______________

DIRECTIONS Reread "Storm Chasers." Then, read the prompt and respond on the lines below.

SCORE

___ / 4

Would you like to take a storm-chasing tour? Explain your answer.

NAME: ______________________________ **DATE:** ________________

DIRECTIONS Read the text and then answer the questions.

When construction started for a new shopping center, Brian couldn't resist going there. What really interested him was the ground where the building was going to be. There might be something interesting buried there.

He was looking closely when one of the workmen called to him, "Hey, get away from there! It's not safe near that equipment."

"Sorry," Brian replied. He was just about to leave when he saw something small, round, and glittering. He picked up a very old-looking coin! On his way out, a worker asked what he had found.

"Just a really old coin," Brian answered. He showed it to the crew leader, who said, "You might have something valuable. You should find out about it."

1. What did Brian find at the construction site?

- (A) an old coin
- (B) a diamond
- (C) a shovel
- (D) nothing

2. What is the setting?

- (A) school
- (B) Brian's house
- (C) a construction site
- (D) a playground

3. The root word in *valuable* is

- (A) value
- (B) val
- (C) able
- (D) lu

4. What does *glittering* mean?

- (A) ugly
- (B) shiny
- (C) small
- (D) hidden

5. *Couldn't resist* hints that Brian

- (A) lives near a construction site.
- (B) does not know about the construction site.
- (C) is afraid of the construction site.
- (D) really wants to go to the construction site.

SCORE

1. Ⓨ Ⓝ
2. Ⓨ Ⓝ
3. Ⓨ Ⓝ
4. Ⓨ Ⓝ
5. Ⓨ Ⓝ

___ / 5 **Total**

NAME: ______________________________ **DATE:** ____________________

DIRECTIONS Read the text and then answer the questions.

SCORE

1. Ⓨ Ⓝ

2. Ⓨ Ⓝ

3. Ⓨ Ⓝ

4. Ⓨ Ⓝ

5. Ⓨ Ⓝ

___ / 5

Total

Brian had found an interesting old coin at a construction site. He took it home to see if he could find out more about it. When he got home, he showed the coin to his parents.

"Do you think it's worth anything?" he asked his father.

"I don't know an awful lot about coins," Dad replied, "but we can do some research to try to find out."

Brian and his father searched online to see if they could find a coin that matched the one Brian had discovered. After a while, they finally found a match. The coin they saw online was worth five hundred dollars! Dad and Brian decided to take Brian's coin to a coin dealer and see if it was valuable.

1. What do Brian and his father discover about the coin online?

- Ⓐ It is worth five hundred dollars.
- Ⓑ It is from Europe.
- Ⓒ It is not valuable.
- Ⓓ It is gold.

2. What is the main setting?

- Ⓐ the coin dealer
- Ⓑ Brian's friend's house
- Ⓒ Brian's construction site
- Ⓓ Brian's home

3. Which is a homophone of *site*?

- Ⓐ sight
- Ⓑ kite
- Ⓒ light
- Ⓓ see

4. Which is a synonym for *site*?

- Ⓐ place
- Ⓑ vision
- Ⓒ machine
- Ⓓ thing

5. In the text, Brian's father says *an awful lot* to tell that he

- Ⓐ does not know about coins.
- Ⓑ knows about coins.
- Ⓒ dislikes coins.
- Ⓓ none of the above

NAME: ______________________ **DATE:** ______________

DIRECTIONS Read the text and then answer the questions.

Brian had found an old coin, so he and his dad went to a coin shop.

"What can I do for you?" the coin dealer asked as he greeted them.

"I found this coin yesterday, and I'm wondering if it's valuable," Brian said.

"Let me examine it, and we'll see what it might be worth," said the dealer.

"How can you tell whether a coin is valuable?" Brian wondered.

"Three of the things we consider are the year the coin was made, the coin's condition, and the mint mark. That's a special symbol that shows where the coin was made," said the coin dealer.

1. Which is **not** considered when determining the value of a coin?

- Ⓐ who owns it
- Ⓑ the year it was made
- Ⓒ the coin's condition
- Ⓓ the mint mark

2. The coin dealer's dialogue shows that he is

- Ⓐ serious about viewing the coin.
- Ⓑ lazy about viewing the coin.
- Ⓒ unsure of how to figure the value of the coin.
- Ⓓ thinking of going home.

3. Which shows the correct pronunciation of *special*?

- Ⓐ SPESH-uhl
- Ⓑ spesh-UHL
- Ⓒ SPECK-ee-uhl
- Ⓓ spesh-EE-uhl

4. An antonym of *condition* is

- Ⓐ state.
- Ⓑ characteristic.
- Ⓒ metal.
- Ⓓ none of the above

5. From which point of view is the story told?

- Ⓐ first person
- Ⓑ second person
- Ⓒ third person
- Ⓓ none of the above

SCORE

1. Ⓨ Ⓝ
2. Ⓨ Ⓝ
3. Ⓨ Ⓝ
4. Ⓨ Ⓝ
5. Ⓨ Ⓝ

___ / 5
Total

NAME: ______________________________ **DATE:** __________________

BRIAN FINDS A TREASURE

Brian and his father were at Center City Coin Shop. They had first visited the shop a few days earlier when Brian found an old coin. He wanted to know whether the coin was valuable, and the dealer had promised to look it up. Today, they would find out whether the coin was worth a lot of money. After the dealer greeted them, he said, "I found out some information about your coin."

"That's great," Brian's father said. "I hope you've got some good news for us."

"Well," said the dealer, "the first thing I did was look up the year the coin was minted, or made. You've got a very old coin here—it's more than 150 years old! I also examined your coin's mint mark. There are several mints in the United States, and they all make coins. Each one has a special symbol called a *mint mark* that it puts on the coins it makes. You can look at any coin and tell by the mint mark which mint made that coin. I found that your coin was minted in Philadelphia. Finally, I looked at the coin to check its condition. Coins that are in perfect condition are called 'mint condition.' They look like they just came from the mint. Coins in mint condition are worth more than coins that are worn. Your coin isn't in mint condition, but it is in very good shape."

"So, how much is my coin worth?" Brian asked eagerly.

"I did some research and found that coins like yours can sell for three hundred dollars."

"Wow! That means you'll give me three hundred dollars for it, right?" Brian said happily.

"What it really means is that I will probably be able to sell it for three hundred dollars. Since I need to earn a profit, how about if I buy your coin for two hundred dollars?"

Brian and his father agreed to the deal, and Brian's father filled out the papers. In no time, Brian had two hundred dollars to put in his bank account.

NAME: ____________________ **DATE:** ____________

DIRECTIONS Read "Brian Finds a Treasure" and then answer the questions.

1. How much money does Brian get for his coin?
   - (A) three hundred dollars
   - (B) five hundred dollars
   - (C) two hundred dollars
   - (D) nothing

2. The purpose for this text is
   - (A) to read a fictional account about coin dealing.
   - (B) to learn everything there is to know about coin dealing.
   - (C) to read a nonfictional account about coin dealing.
   - (D) all of the above

3. Where will Brian and his father probably go to next?
   - (A) another coin dealer
   - (B) a movie
   - (C) the grocery store
   - (D) the bank

4. How does Brian probably feel about finding out the worth of the coin?
   - (A) upset
   - (B) nervous
   - (C) excited
   - (D) furious

5. How do coin dealers determine the value of coins?
   - (A) by deciding whether they like the coin's owner
   - (B) by asking a friend
   - (C) by looking at their year, mint mark, and condition
   - (D) by making them mint condition

6. This text is an example of
   - (A) a character discovering fortune after a lot of hard work.
   - (B) a character discovering fortune without trying to.
   - (C) detailed coin-dealing strategy and how to make a living with coins.
   - (D) all of the above

SCORE

1. Ⓨ Ⓝ
2. Ⓨ Ⓝ
3. Ⓨ Ⓝ
4. Ⓨ Ⓝ
5. Ⓨ Ⓝ
6. Ⓨ Ⓝ

___ / 6 Total

NAME: ______________________ **DATE:** ______________

DIRECTIONS Reread "Brian Finds a Treasure." Then, read the prompt and respond on the lines below.

SCORE

___ / 4

What would you do if you found a valuable coin? Write about what you would do.

NAME: ____________________ **DATE:** ____________

DIRECTIONS Read the text and then answer the questions.

Glass painting is a special kind of painting. Artists who paint on glass use special paints. Those paints let them create beautiful pictures on the glass. Then, when sunlight comes through the glass, the colors seem to come alive. Some artists do reverse glass painting. They paint their pictures backward, beginning with the finishing touches. Next, they paint the main details. Then, they paint the background. When the painting is finished, it dries. Then, you can see the picture through the other side of the glass. Stained glass is a kind of glass painting, too. Artists who make stained glass use another kind of paint. After the artist applies the paint, the glass is heated to bond the paint to the glass. That is why it is called stained glass.

1. What does *reverse glass painting* mean?

Ⓐ to paint on anything except glass
Ⓑ to paint when it is sunny
Ⓒ to paint with the opposite hand
Ⓓ to paint backward, starting with the finishing touches

2. In which chapter of a book on painting would this text most likely be found?

Ⓐ The Still Life
Ⓑ Portraits
Ⓒ Glass Techniques
Ⓓ Palette Design

3. Which word does not have a long *a* vowel sound?

Ⓐ artist
Ⓑ stained
Ⓒ painting
Ⓓ create

4. *Reverse* and *backward* are

Ⓐ synonyms.
Ⓑ antonyms.
Ⓒ rhymes.
Ⓓ opposites.

5. *The colors seem to come alive* is an example of

Ⓐ rhyme.
Ⓑ personification.
Ⓒ simile.
Ⓓ fable.

SCORE

1. Ⓨ Ⓝ
2. Ⓨ Ⓝ
3. Ⓨ Ⓝ
4. Ⓨ Ⓝ
5. Ⓨ Ⓝ

___ / 5
Total

NAME: ______________________ **DATE:** ______________

DIRECTIONS Read the text and then answer the questions.

SCORE

1. Ⓨ Ⓝ
2. Ⓨ Ⓝ
3. Ⓨ Ⓝ
4. Ⓨ Ⓝ
5. Ⓨ Ⓝ

___ / 5 Total

Glass painting is a very old art form. Nobody knows exactly when people began to paint glass. But painted glass figures have been found in the ruins of ancient Rome. Glass painting became very important during the 10th century. At that time, people were building churches, and painted glass was used for the windows. The pictures in the glass windows were used to tell stories. As time went on, people learned new ways to paint glass and made new kinds of paints. So glass painting changed. Today, glass painting artists do not paint just windows. And they do not just tell stories with their pictures. Glass painting is used on all sorts of things, such as dishes, vases, and drinking glasses.

1. Which is **not** a true statement about glass paintings?

Ⓐ It became important during the 10th century.

Ⓑ It is an old art form.

Ⓒ It can be done on windows, dishes, vases, and glasses.

Ⓓ It is for glass that is too small to paint.

2. What is the purpose of glass painting on windows in churches?

Ⓐ to make churches pretty

Ⓑ to show off new artists

Ⓒ to hide broken windows

Ⓓ to tell stories

3. Which is a homophone of *new*?

Ⓐ fresh

Ⓑ old

Ⓒ knew

Ⓓ kinds

4. *Ancient* is a synonym for

Ⓐ expensive.

Ⓑ royal.

Ⓒ old.

Ⓓ Western.

5. Which two words describe the tone of the text?

Ⓐ *argumentative* and *serious*

Ⓑ *informative* and *silly*

Ⓒ *informative* and *serious*

Ⓓ *interesting* and *hurried*

NAME: ______________________ **DATE:** ______________

DIRECTIONS Read the text and then answer the questions.

While it's true that glass painting started in Europe, it didn't stay local for long. Glass painting spread to India, China, Africa, and the United States, too. Today, there are glass paintings all over the world. Each place has its own style. Many Indian glass paintings have very bright colors. They may have fancy patterns. Chinese glass paintings use both dark colors and light colors. They may show flowers. They may show birds and other animals. Beautiful African glass paintings show daily life. Some are used to teach lessons. They often use bold, bright colors. What about the United States? There are a lot of beautiful glass paintings in the United States, too!

1. After reading the text, a reader would most benefit by looking at examples of stained glass
   - (A) from China.
   - (B) from India.
   - (C) from different cultures.
   - (D) from the United States.

2. Which images are not on Chinese glass paintings?
   - (A) airplanes
   - (B) flowers
   - (C) birds
   - (D) all of the above

3. Which word has the same vowel sound as the word *style*?
   - (A) bright
   - (B) African
   - (C) stay
   - (D) beautiful

4. The root word in *daily* is
   - (A) dai.
   - (B) dail.
   - (C) day.
   - (D) ily.

5. What is the author's purpose?
   - (A) to inform
   - (B) to entertain
   - (C) to persuade
   - (D) to instruct

SCORE

1. (Y)(N)
2. (Y)(N)
3. (Y)(N)
4. (Y)(N)
5. (Y)(N)

___ / 5 Total

NAME: ______________________ **DATE:** ______________

MAKE YOUR OWN PAINTED GLASS

It's easy to make your own beautiful painted glass picture. Here's what you will need:

- A picture frame
- White glue
- Glass paint and brushes
- Coloring book page or drawing
- Tape or a hot-glue gun

Here is what you'll need to do:

1. Draw a picture, or if you'd prefer, choose a picture from a coloring book.
2. Remove the back of the picture frame.
3. Using tape or a hot-glue gun, secure the glass in the frame from the back.
4. Place the frame facedown over your picture.
5. Using the glass paints and brushes, color in your picture.
6. Squeeze out $\frac{1}{3}$ of the glue and replace it with black paint. Mix them together.
7. Using the original glue container, squeeze paint and glue mixture to line your picture to give it a stained-glass effect.
8. Let your picture dry.
9. Then, replace the back and hang your picture on the wall or attach strings to hang it in a window without the backing.

NAME: ____________________ **DATE:** ____________

DIRECTIONS Read "Make Your Own Painted Glass" and then answer the questions.

1. Why do you think you need glass paint for this project?

   Ⓐ Glass paint has brighter colors.
   Ⓑ Other kinds of paint might not work properly on glass.
   Ⓒ Glass paint is easier to find than other kinds of paint.
   Ⓓ Other kinds of paint do not come in as many colors.

2. You might read this if you wanted to

   Ⓐ find out about stained-glass windows.
   Ⓑ learn about African glass art.
   Ⓒ try a glass painting project.
   Ⓓ find out where to buy glass paintings.

3. Which is the first step in making your own painted glass?

   Ⓐ Draw or choose a picture.
   Ⓑ Paint the glass.
   Ⓒ Use tape to secure the glass in the frame.
   Ⓓ Let the picture dry.

4. Adding the stained-glass effect comes after

   Ⓐ coloring in the picture.
   Ⓑ letting the picture dry.
   Ⓒ replacing the back.
   Ⓓ hanging the picture in a window.

5. This would be interesting to people who like

   Ⓐ mathematics.
   Ⓑ science.
   Ⓒ art.
   Ⓓ history.

6. What is a good summary of this text?

   Ⓐ This tells what glass painting is.
   Ⓑ This tells how to squeeze glue.
   Ⓒ This tells where glass painting started.
   Ⓓ This tells how to make your own glass painting.

SCORE

1. Ⓨ Ⓝ
2. Ⓨ Ⓝ
3. Ⓨ Ⓝ
4. Ⓨ Ⓝ
5. Ⓨ Ⓝ
6. Ⓨ Ⓝ

___ / 6
Total

NAME: ______________________ **DATE:** ______________

DIRECTIONS Reread "Make Your Own Painted Glass." Then, read the prompt and respond on the lines below.

SCORE

___ / 4

Which step would be hardest for you? Which step would be easiest? Why? Explain your answer.

NAME: ______________________ **DATE:** ______________

DIRECTIONS Read the text and then answer the questions.

Luis called excitedly, "Mom, I want to show you something I found online! I found *The Secret of the Magician* and *The Crystal Cavern*! I've been looking for those movies forever! Can we order them?"

Luis's mom looked closely at the website Luis was showing her. "It looks as though this *Movies and More* website has just about everything," she said.

"The prices are cheap," Luis assured her. "Can we please order them?"

His mom checked the site to be sure it was safe and then nodded and said, "I'll get my credit card, and we'll order them."

1. Why is Luis excited?

- (A) His mom found a good price on a website.
- (B) He found the movies he wants.
- (C) He gets to have a credit card.
- (D) He gets a new computer.

2. Why does Luis's mom look at the safety of the site?

- (A) because she doesn't want Luis to get hurt
- (B) to make sure her credit card information won't be stolen
- (C) to find emergency kits
- (D) to make sure there are no strangers in chat rooms

3. In the word *closely*, close is the

- (A) root word.
- (B) prefix.
- (C) suffix.
- (D) affix.

4. Which is a synonym for *cheap*?

- (A) expensive
- (B) costly
- (C) affordable
- (D) all of the above

5. *I've been looking for those movies forever* is an example of

- (A) an idiom.
- (B) hyperbole.
- (C) a metaphor.
- (D) a simile.

SCORE

1. (Y)(N)
2. (Y)(N)
3. (Y)(N)
4. (Y)(N)
5. (Y)(N)

___ / 5
Total

NAME: ______________________ **DATE:** ______________

DIRECTIONS Read the text and then answer the questions.

SCORE

1. Ⓨ Ⓝ

2. Ⓨ Ⓝ

3. Ⓨ Ⓝ

4. Ⓨ Ⓝ

5. Ⓨ Ⓝ

___ / 5 Total

After school, Luis raced home from the bus stop at top speed. His mother had ordered two movies for him, and he was eager to see if they'd arrived. So far, the answer had been, "No, they haven't." Today, Luis rushed home as usual and burst through the door. "Are they here yet?" he called out.

"The mail's lying over there on the coffee table," his mother answered. "Why don't you check it out for yourself and see if your movies are here?"

When Luis grabbed the mail, the first thing he saw was a package addressed to him. He ripped open the wrapper and pulled out the packaging material. Out fell the two movies. "They're finally here!" he yelled happily.

1. Which title best fits the text?

Ⓐ The Mail
Ⓑ Expecting the Package
Ⓒ Movies
Ⓓ Asking Mom

2. The setting flows from

Ⓐ the bus stop to the movie store.
Ⓑ the bus stop to Luis's home.
Ⓒ Luis's home to the bus stop.
Ⓓ none of the above

3. Which words have the same root word?

Ⓐ *package* and *packaging*
Ⓑ *ripped* and *wrapper*
Ⓒ *yelled* and *pulled*
Ⓓ *haven't* and *they'd*

4. Which verb tells you that Luis moved very quickly?

Ⓐ *called*
Ⓑ *arrived*
Ⓒ *ordered*
Ⓓ *rushed*

5. *As usual* means

Ⓐ like most days.
Ⓑ just this once.
Ⓒ for the first time.
Ⓓ anxiously.

NAME: ____________________ **DATE:** ____________

DIRECTIONS Read the text and then answer the questions.

Luis and his friends Tom and Dave were going to watch Luis's new movies. The boys had popcorn and lemonade. They voted to watch *The Crystal Cavern* first, but when Luis put the DVD in the player, nothing happened.

"Let's just watch the other movie for now," Dave suggested. Luis put *The Secret of the Magician* into the player, but it didn't play either.

"I don't know if the problem is the movies or our player," Luis said. "I'm going to put in one of our other movies and see if it works." When he put in another movie, it worked perfectly.

"Neither of my new movies works," Luis said. "I need to send them back!"

1. How do Luis and his friends decide which movie to watch first?

Ⓐ they vote
Ⓑ they let Luis choose
Ⓒ Luis's mom chooses
Ⓓ they argue

2. Why does Luis have to send the movies back?

Ⓐ Luis does not like the movies.
Ⓑ Luis's player is broken.
Ⓒ They are the wrong movies.
Ⓓ The movies do not work.

3. *Magician* is pronounced

Ⓐ MAG-ick-ahn
Ⓑ muh-GICK-ahn
Ⓒ muh-gish-UHN
Ⓓ none of the above

4. Which is an antonym of *neither*?

Ⓐ some
Ⓑ both
Ⓒ any
Ⓓ all

5. To say that something works *perfectly* means

Ⓐ that it will break soon.
Ⓑ that something is broken.
Ⓒ that something works exactly right.
Ⓓ that something will work forever.

SCORE

1. ⓎⓃ
2. ⓎⓃ
3. ⓎⓃ
4. ⓎⓃ
5. ⓎⓃ

___ / 5
Total

NAME: ______________________ **DATE:** ______________

SENDING IT BACK

Luis's mother had ordered two new movies for him. One was *The Secret of the Magician,* and the other was *The Crystal Cavern*. Luis was excited about the new movies, but when he tried to watch them, neither movie worked. He knew he would have to send them back, but he wasn't sure how to go about it. So he asked his mother to help.

"The first step," she told him, "is to go to the company's website. We bought the movies from *Movies and More*, so let's start by going to that site." Luis and his mother pulled up chairs by the computer, and Luis found the site.

"Now," said his mother, "see if you can find a place for questions about orders." Luis found a section called *Orders and Shipping*, and clicked on that link. That section had instructions for returning merchandise. Luis and his mother read the instructions.

The first thing they did was complete a return form. After Luis and his mother completed that form, they were ready to print a return label. They printed the label and got a box. Then, Luis put the movies in the box and sealed it up. Luis and his mother took the box and the label to the post office, where the label was attached to the box.

"Now what happens?" Luis asked his mother as they prepared to go home. His mother replied, "The next thing that will happen is that the company will get the movies back. Then, they'll send us new copies of the movies."

"How long is that going to take?" Luis wanted to know.

"The website says the process takes two to four weeks, so it's not going to happen immediately. But it won't be awfully long," his mother answered. And she was right. Three weeks later, Luis got brand-new copies of *The Secret of the Magician* and *The Crystal Cavern*, and this time, they worked!

NAME: ______________________ **DATE:** ______________

DIRECTIONS Read "Sending It Back" and then answer the questions.

1. This text is

(A) a fictional, unrealistic account of how to return an item ordered online.

(B) a fictional, realistic account of how to return an item ordered online.

(C) nonfiction and is meant to describe how an Internet company works.

(D) nonfiction and is meant to describe how to return things.

2. The author has probably

(A) experienced a broken product and had to return it.

(B) never returned anything.

(C) returned all sorts of things through the mail.

(D) been sailing around the world.

3. If only one of the movies had not worked, Luis would have

(A) returned only the broken movie.

(B) been happy with just the one movie.

(C) taken a bus to the movie company.

(D) returned both movies, just to be sure.

4. How does Luis probably feel about having to send back his movies?

(A) excited

(B) disappointed

(C) jealous

(D) proud

5. What is probably true about Luis?

(A) He is used to computers.

(B) He does not like movies.

(C) He is angry with his mother.

(D) He does not like to ask questions.

6. This text is an example of

(A) a character with a problem but no solution.

(B) a character resolving problems for other characters.

(C) a character creating a conflict for other characters to solve.

(D) a character experiencing a conflict and then resolving it.

SCORE

1. (Y) (N)

2. (Y) (N)

3. (Y) (N)

4. (Y) (N)

5. (Y) (N)

6. (Y) (N)

___ / 6
Total

NAME: ______________________________ **DATE:** ________________

SCORE

___ / 4

DIRECTIONS Reread "Sending It Back." Then, read the prompt and respond on the lines below.

Have you ever had to send anything back? Write about what happened.

NAME: ______________________ **DATE:** ______________

DIRECTIONS Read the text and then answer the questions.

"What time is it?" That sounds like an easy question to answer, but it isn't. The answer depends on where you live. Earth rotates on its axis, so the sun strikes different parts of it at different times. There are twenty-four time zones in the world. As you go east, it gets later; as you go west, it gets earlier. So it is earlier in Chicago than it is in New York. But it is later in Chicago than it is in Los Angeles. When it's the middle of the afternoon in Europe, people in California are just waking up. When it's breakfast time in New York, it's almost lunchtime in London. So, next time you're sitting in class and feeling hungry because it's lunchtime, think about it. Somewhere else in the world, kids are getting ready to go to bed. Other kids in other places are just waking up.

1. Which image would help a reader understand the text?

- (A) a globe of the Earth
- (B) a map of the Earth's oceans
- (C) a map of the Earth's time zones
- (D) a map of Chicago and New York

2. Which sentence best summarizes the text?

- (A) As you go east, it gets later; as you go west, it gets earlier.
- (B) The answer depends on where you live.
- (C) There are twenty-four time zones in the world.
- (D) Other kids in other places are just waking up.

3. Which word is **not** plural?

- (A) axis
- (B) kids
- (C) places
- (D) zones

4. Another word for *rotates* is

- (A) grows.
- (B) opens.
- (C) follows.
- (D) turns.

5. The phrase *the sun strikes* means that

- (A) the sun runs out of fuel.
- (B) the sun shines on.
- (C) the sun is violent.
- (D) the sun is round.

SCORE

1. Ⓨ Ⓝ

2. Ⓨ Ⓝ

3. Ⓨ Ⓝ

4. Ⓨ Ⓝ

5. Ⓨ Ⓝ

___ / 5

Total

NAME: ______________________ DATE: ______________

DIRECTIONS Read the text and then answer the questions.

SCORE

1. Ⓨ Ⓝ

2. Ⓨ Ⓝ

3. Ⓨ Ⓝ

4. Ⓨ Ⓝ

5. Ⓨ Ⓝ

___ / 5
Total

Imagine you fly around the world starting from New York. You fly through all twenty-four time zones on Earth. You fly west, so it gets earlier as you go. You gain an hour each time you pass through a time zone. Now, imagine you have flown all around the world and you land back in New York. Remember that you lost an hour each time you flew through a time zone. Does that mean you land on the same day you left? No—you have been in the plane for twenty-four hours, so it is a day later. How can that be, if you lost an hour for each time zone? The answer is the International Date Line. The International Date Line is an imaginary line like the equator. It runs from north to south through the Pacific Ocean. This line divides one day from the next day. So if it is Wednesday on the east side of the line, it is Tuesday on the west side.

1. Which title best fits the text?

Ⓐ The International Date Line
Ⓑ Date Line
Ⓒ Same Day You Left
Ⓓ Arriving Where You Started

2. What happens as you fly west?

Ⓐ You get motion sickness.
Ⓑ You gain an hour at each time zone.
Ⓒ You fly too fast.
Ⓓ You go to the wrong place.

3. Which syllable is stressed in the word *imaginary*?

Ⓐ the first syllable
Ⓑ the second syllable
Ⓒ the third syllable
Ⓓ the fourth syllable

4. *Earlier* and *later* are

Ⓐ antonyms.
Ⓑ synonyms.
Ⓒ rhymes.
Ⓓ nouns.

5. The author most likely wrote this to

Ⓐ entertain an audience and talk about time.
Ⓑ inform an audience about the International Date Line.
Ⓒ talk about the Pacific Ocean and imaginary lines.
Ⓓ remind you to wear a watch when flying.

NAME: ______________________ **DATE:** ______________

DIRECTIONS Read the text and then answer the questions.

How did time zones start? Why were they created? Long ago, each small community had a different way of using the sun to keep time. When people began to use trains, this became a problem. There was no good way to make a train schedule. And so each community kept time in a different way. Sir Sandford Fleming was a Canadian railroad planner. He came up with a solution to this problem. His idea was a system of time zones that everyone would use. Each town's time zone would depend on where it was located. In 1884, people from twenty-seven countries had a meeting in Washington, DC. They decided where those time zones would be. Now, the world is divided into twenty-four time zones. No matter where you are going, you can know what time it will be when you get there.

1. After reading the first sentence, a reader might predict that

- Ⓐ the text will be about how time zones were decided upon.
- Ⓑ the text will discuss why time zones were needed.
- Ⓒ the text will be about the creation of time zones.
- Ⓓ all of the above

2. If this were found in a book on keeping time, what chapter might it be found in?

- Ⓐ The Need for International Time
- Ⓑ The Rise of the Digital Clock
- Ⓒ Measuring Time with Precision
- Ⓓ Trains Know the Time

3. The root word in *countries* is

- Ⓐ count.
- Ⓑ country.
- Ⓒ county.
- Ⓓ none of the above

4. *Came up with* means

- Ⓐ did not like.
- Ⓑ could not think of.
- Ⓒ thought of.
- Ⓓ asked for.

5. What is the author's purpose?

- Ⓐ to persuade
- Ⓑ to entertain
- Ⓒ to instruct
- Ⓓ to inform

SCORE

1. Ⓨ Ⓝ
2. Ⓨ Ⓝ
3. Ⓨ Ⓝ
4. Ⓨ Ⓝ
5. Ⓨ Ⓝ

___ / 5 Total

NAME: ______________________ **DATE:** ______________

WHAT TIME IS IT?

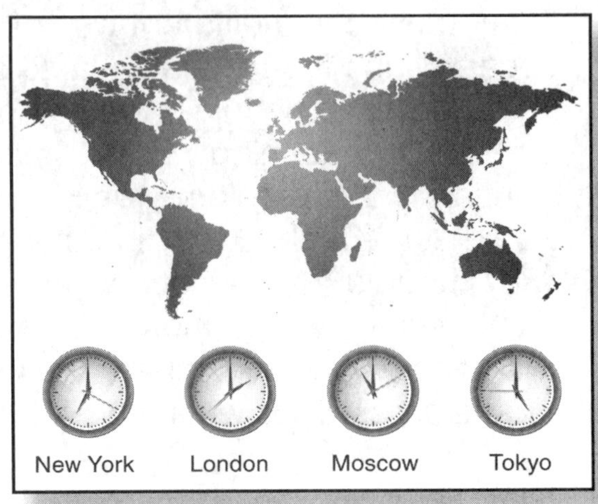

Today, cars, trains, and airplanes go all over the world. They cross every time zone. There are twenty-four standard time zones in the world. Those zones are divided by time zone lines. Time zone lines are imaginary, like the International Date Line. So you cannot see them when you cross them. But they separate one time zone from the next. Time zone lines run from north to south. Places that are in the same time zone have the same time. Even places that are far away from each other might have the same time if they are in the same time zone. For example, Mexico City is in Mexico, and Winnipeg is in Canada. They are very far apart. But it's the same time in Mexico City as it is in Winnipeg; they are in the same time zone.

Many places change their clocks twice a year. In the spring, clocks are moved forward by one hour. That's called *daylight saving time*. In the autumn, people set their clocks back again to standard time. People do this because in many parts of the world, days get longer during the summer. Setting clocks ahead allows people to have more daylight at the end of the day.

This chart shows the time in some other places when it is noon on Thursday in Los Angeles.

City, Country	Day	Time
Los Angeles, United States	Thursday	12:00 P.M.
Mexico City, Mexico	Thursday	2:00 P.M.
New York, United States	Thursday	3:00 P.M.
La Paz, Bolivia	Thursday	3:00 P.M.
London, England	Thursday	8:00 P.M.
Cairo, Egypt	Thursday	9:00 P.M.
Moscow, Russia	Thursday	11:00 P.M.
Auckland, New Zealand	Friday	8:00 A.M.

NAME: ____________________ **DATE:** ____________

DIRECTIONS Read "What Time Is It?" and then answer the questions.

1. What does the chart at the end of the article show?

- Ⓐ only cities in North America
- Ⓑ a train schedule
- Ⓒ the times at different locations
- Ⓓ a calendar

2. The purpose for reading this text is mostly

- Ⓐ to learn about the different time zones in the world.
- Ⓑ to learn about the International Date Line.
- Ⓒ to learn about moving clocks forward in the springtime.
- Ⓓ to learn about clocks.

3. When are clocks moved forward an hour?

- Ⓐ in the spring
- Ⓑ at standard time
- Ⓒ in the winter
- Ⓓ on Thursdays

4. If there were no time zones, then

- Ⓐ it would only cause small problems during travel.
- Ⓑ no one could tell what time it was as they traveled the globe.
- Ⓒ discussing when to do things with people who live far away would be easier.
- Ⓓ nothing would change; they aren't very useful.

5. What is the main idea?

- Ⓐ Airplanes travel all over the world.
- Ⓑ It is Thursday in Mexico City.
- Ⓒ Daylight savings time happens in the spring.
- Ⓓ There are twenty-four hour time zones.

6. From the chart, it is _______ in Cairo than it is in London.

- Ⓐ later
- Ⓑ cooler
- Ⓒ earlier
- Ⓓ sooner

SCORE

1. Ⓨ Ⓝ
2. Ⓨ Ⓝ
3. Ⓨ Ⓝ
4. Ⓨ Ⓝ
5. Ⓨ Ⓝ
6. Ⓨ Ⓝ

___ / 6 **Total**

NAME: ______________________ **DATE:** ______________

DIRECTIONS Reread "What Time Is It?" Then, read the prompt and respond on the lines below.

SCORE

___ / 4

Daylight saving time began as a way to make use of daylight before we had electricity. Write about whether we still need daylight saving time today.

NAME: ____________________ **DATE:** ____________

DIRECTIONS Read the text and then answer the questions.

Morgan enjoyed summer vacation, but after a while, she began to get bored. Then, she thought it might be fun to have some sort of job. The problem with that was that there weren't many jobs available for fourth-graders. One day, Morgan's mother was getting ready to go to work. She was a photographer, and Morgan had always thought her work must be interesting. As she watched Mom gather her things, Morgan said, "I wish I could go to work, too, and learn photography."

"Would you like to?" Mom asked. "If you want to, you could come along with me and help out while you're on vacation."

"That would be amazing!" Morgan answered. "I've always wondered what it'd be like."

1. Which phrase suggests that Morgan will start looking for things to do?

- (A) she began to get bored
- (B) chores for her to do
- (C) if she told her parents
- (D) ready to go to work

2. After Morgan and her mother leave the house, which will be the most likely setting?

- (A) the waiting line at the bank
- (B) an office with desks and computers
- (C) a photo shoot with props and models
- (D) an alien spaceship

3. Which word does not have a long *a* vowel sound?

- (A) vacation
- (B) always
- (C) Morgan
- (D) amazing

4. What is a synonym for *gather*?

- (A) collect
- (B) lose
- (C) buy
- (D) scatter

5. *After a while* means

- (A) not right away.
- (B) immediately.
- (C) the next day.
- (D) never.

SCORE

1. Ⓨ Ⓝ

2. Ⓨ Ⓝ

3. Ⓨ Ⓝ

4. Ⓨ Ⓝ

5. Ⓨ Ⓝ

___ / 5

Total

NAME: ______________________ **DATE:** ______________

DIRECTIONS Read the text and then answer the questions.

SCORE

1. Ⓨ Ⓝ
2. Ⓨ Ⓝ
3. Ⓨ Ⓝ
4. Ⓨ Ⓝ
5. Ⓨ Ⓝ

___ / 5
Total

Morgan and her mother got to the photography studio at 9:00 A.M. Her mom worked at the studio, and Morgan was going to help out for the summer. When they got there, Morgan's mom showed her where to put her things. Then, she gave Morgan a tour of the studio. There were two equipment rooms. That was where the photographers kept their cameras. There were three rooms for taking pictures. Those rooms had little stages with props such as chairs and boxes. They had cloth of different colors, too, to use as backgrounds in pictures. There were also big boxes of toys to make babies smile and laugh in their pictures. Finally, her mom showed Morgan the computers. She said they were used to store pictures.

1. Which image would best help a reader to visualize the setting?

Ⓐ an image of a photo studio
Ⓑ an image of a photographer
Ⓒ a picture taken in the studio
Ⓓ a picture of a large movie set

2. Which genre is this text?

Ⓐ biography
Ⓑ science fiction
Ⓒ realistic fiction
Ⓓ fantasy

3. Which words have the same root word?

Ⓐ *pictures* and *photography*
Ⓑ *photography* and *photographers*
Ⓒ *Morgan* and *mom*
Ⓓ *chairs* and *boxes*

4. In this text, *stages* means

Ⓐ wagons.
Ⓑ parts of a process.
Ⓒ a flat surface to be viewed on.
Ⓓ something animals are kept in.

5. Which word indicates that the computers are the last thing Morgan's mom shows her?

Ⓐ stored
Ⓑ computers
Ⓒ showed
Ⓓ finally

NAME: ____________________ **DATE:** ______________

DIRECTIONS Read the text and then answer the questions.

Morgan was helping out at her mother's photography studio. She knew she wasn't ready to actually take pictures, but she didn't want to just sit and watch. So she asked her mother what she would be doing. She was hoping it would be interesting.

Mom told her, "You can keep the studio rooms clean and organized. That's really important. If they're a mess, people won't want to get their pictures taken. And it will be harder to find the props we need. You can also run errands and call customers when their pictures are ready. Those are important things, too."

"I'm going to be awfully busy," said Morgan. But she didn't mind at all. It all sounded interesting.

1. Which will Morgan **not** do to help her mom?
   - (A) keep the studio clean
   - (B) call customers
   - (C) take pictures
   - (D) run errands

2. When is the text set?
   - (A) in the past
   - (B) in the present
   - (C) in the future
   - (D) it changes during the text from past to future

3. The root word in *organized* is
   - (A) org.
   - (B) organize.
   - (C) ized.
   - (D) organ.

4. A synonym for *ready* is
   - (A) prepared.
   - (B) interested.
   - (C) busy.
   - (D) adult.

5. To *run errands* means
   - (A) to walk to a place.
   - (B) to run a race course.
   - (C) to run through errors.
   - (D) to complete chores and tasks.

SCORE

1. (Y)(N)
2. (Y)(N)
3. (Y)(N)
4. (Y)(N)
5. (Y)(N)

___ / 5
Total

NAME: ______________________________ **DATE:** ________________

SMILE FOR THE CAMERA!

Morgan was helping out at her mother's photography studio. She had been working there and learning for a few weeks. Her mom said that Morgan did a great job. The other photographers agreed. One day, Morgan asked her mom if she could help take a picture.

"I know I'm not ready to use the equipment by myself," she said, "but could I at least help?"

"I suppose so," her mom said. "I have a family coming in at noon today. You can help with that photo session."

Morgan was excited to meet the family and get started. When they got there, her mom introduced herself. She also introduced Morgan. Then, they started to plan the pictures. The first thing to think about was how many people would be in the pictures. There were five people in this family. They also had to think about the ages of the children. There were three kids, and one was a baby. So Morgan guessed they would use toys to make the baby smile.

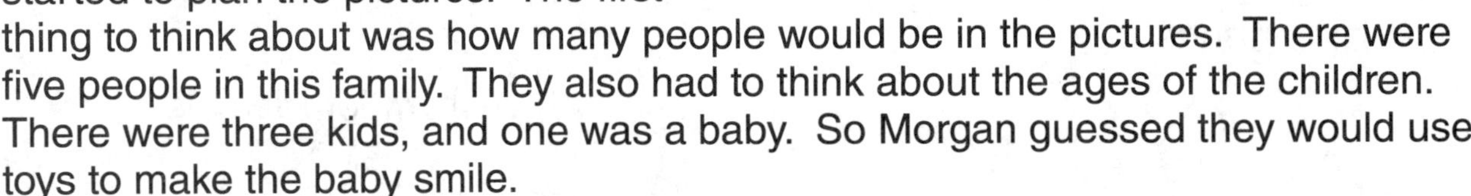

Now it was time to choose the background. Morgan and her mom talked to the family about which color they wanted. The family wanted a light color; her mom thought that was a good idea. So Morgan suggested pale blue. Everyone said that was the right choice. Next, her mom got the camera. When the camera was set up, her mom had the family sit in several different poses. She took pictures of each pose. While her mom took the pictures, Morgan used some toys to make the baby laugh and smile. When her mom was done, she asked the family to wait for a few minutes. Then, she put the film disc in the computer and made a file with all the poses. Morgan told the family when her mom was ready for them. Then, the family chose the pictures they wanted. Morgan wrote down their order on an order form. The family thanked Morgan and her mom and left. Her mom said, "You did a super job, Morgan! Maybe you'll be a photographer yourself when you're older."

NAME: ______________________ **DATE:** ______________

DIRECTIONS Read "Smile for the Camera!" and then answer the questions.

1. What does Morgan **not** do to help with the photo shoot?

- (A) helps choose a background
- (B) gets lunch for everyone
- (C) makes the baby laugh
- (D) writes down the family's order

2. What is the author's purpose?

- (A) to inform
- (B) to entertain
- (C) to persuade
- (D) to instruct

3. How might this story be different if there were no babies in the family?

- (A) Morgan would not use toys.
- (B) Her mom would not get the camera.
- (C) The family would not want a light background.
- (D) Morgan would not write the family's order on an order form.

4. How does Morgan probably feel when her mom says she did a super job?

- (A) proud
- (B) curious
- (C) angry
- (D) jealous

5. People who like ______ might want to be photographers.

- (A) history
- (B) mathematics
- (C) art
- (D) cooking

6. Which summarizes the theme of this text?

- (A) It is good to do something that is difficult.
- (B) You can be rewarded for not doing a very good job.
- (C) You can earn trust after putting in hard work.
- (D) It is helpful to ignore the things you really want.

SCORE

1. Ⓨ Ⓝ
2. Ⓨ Ⓝ
3. Ⓨ Ⓝ
4. Ⓨ Ⓝ
5. Ⓨ Ⓝ
6. Ⓨ Ⓝ

___ / 6
Total

NAME: ______________________ **DATE:** ______________

DIRECTIONS Reread "Smile for the Camera!" Then, read the prompt and respond on the lines below.

SCORE

___ / 4

Think about a time when you had your picture taken. What was it like? Write about what happened.

ANSWER KEY

Week 1

Day 1
1. B
2. D
3. B
4. A
5 C

Day 2
1. A
2. A
3. A
4. B
5. D

Day 3
1. B
2. C
3. D
4. A
5. A

Day 4
1. B
2. A
3. C
4. C
5. C
6. A

Day 5
Responses will vary.

Week 2

Day 1
1. A
2. A
3. C
4. B
5. D

Day 2
1. D
2. C
3. A
4. D
5. D

Day 3
1. A
2. D
3. D
4. C
5. D

Day 4
1. C
2. A
3. B
4. C
5. C
6. C

Day 5
Responses will vary.

Week 3

Day 1
1. D
2. D
3. A
4. D
5. B

Day 2
1. C
2. C
3. C
4. A
5. C

Day 3
1. B
2. C
3. D
4. C
5. D

Day 4
1. B
2. B
3. A
4. A
5. C
6. A

Day 5
Responses will vary.

Week 4

Day 1
1. A
2. D
3. D
4. D
5. B

Day 2
1. C
2. D
3. A
4. B
5. C

Day 3
1. C
2. B
3. B
4. A
5. D

Day 4
1. C
2. A
3. B
4. C
5. C
6. D

Day 5
Responses will vary.

Week 5

Day 1
1. D
2. C
3. C
4. A
5. A

Day 2
1. D
2. A
3. A
4. D
5. C

Day 3
1. C
2. D
3. A
4. D
5. B

Day 4
1. C
2. D
3. D
4. A
5. D
6. C

Day 5
Responses will vary.

Week 6

Day 1
1. B
2. D
3. B
4. A
5. B

Day 2
1. A
2. C
3. A
4. D
5. A

Day 3
1. D
2. B
3. D
4. D
5. B

ANSWER KEY *(cont.)*

Week 6 *(cont.)*

Day 4

1. B
2. A
3. C
4. D
5. B
6. A

Day 5

Responses will vary.

Week 7

Day 1

1. B
2. D
3. C
4. A
5. A

Day 2

1. A
2. B
3. B
4. D
5. D

Day 3

1. A
2. D
3. D
4. D
5. C

Day 4

1. C
2. B
3. A
4. C
5. D
6. B

Day 5

Responses will vary.

Week 8

Day 1

1. C
2. B
3. C
4. D
5. A

Day 2

1. D
2. B
3. A
4. B
5. A

Day 3

1. D
2. D
3. D
4. C
5. D

Day 4

1. A
2. C
3. C
4. A
5. B
6. C

Day 5

Responses will vary.

Week 9

Day 1

1. D
2. D
3. C
4. A
5. D

Day 2

1. A
2. D
3. B
4. C
5. B

Day 3

1. C
2. C
3. C
4. D
5. B

Day 4

1. D
2. D
3. C
4. A
5. D
6. B

Day 5

Responses will vary.

Week 10

Day 1

1. B
2. B
3. A
4. D
5. D

Day 2

1. D
2. D
3. C
4. B
5. D

Day 3

1. B
2. B
3. A
4. D
5. C

Day 4

1. B
2. B
3. C
4. A
5. D
6. C

Day 5

Responses will vary.

Week 11

Day 1

1. C
2. B
3. D
4. A
5. D

Day 2

1. A
2. C
3. B
4. B
5. C

Day 3

1. D
2. A
3. A
4. B
5. A

Day 4

1. B
2. D
3. D
4. C
5. C
6. C

Day 5

Responses will vary.

Week 12

Day 1

1. D
2. A
3. B
4. B
5. D

ANSWER KEY *(cont.)*

Week 12 *(cont.)*

Day 2
1. C
2. A
3. D
4. D
5. B

Day 3
1. B
2. D
3. C
4. B
5. B

Day 4
1. D
2. A
3. B
4. B
5. B
6. A

Day 5
Responses will vary.

Week 13

Day 1
1. D
2. B
3. A
4. B
5. D

Day 2
1. A
2. D
3. D
4. D
5. B

Day 3
1. B
2. B
3. C
4. C
5. A

Day 4
1. B
2. C
3. B
4. B
5. A
6. C

Day 5
Responses will vary.

Week 14

Day 1
1. D
2. A
3. B
4. D
5. B

Day 2
1. A
2. C
3. B
4. B
5. B

Day 3
1. B
2. B
3. A
4. D
5. B

Day 4
1. D
2. A
3. C
4. B
5. D
6. A

Day 5
Responses will vary.

Week 15

Day 1
1. B
2. A
3. A
4. D
5. A

Day 2
1. C
2. B
3. D
4. A
5. A

Day 3
1. D
2. B
3. C
4. A
5. B

Day 4
1. D
2. C
3. D
4. A
5. B
6. D

Day 5
Responses will vary.

Week 16

Day 1
1. A
2. C
3. D
4. A
5. D

Day 2
1. B
2. B
3. D
4. B
5. A

Day 3
1. C
2. B
3. C
4. C
5. D

Day 4
1. B
2. A
3. B
4. D
5. D
6. A

Day 5
Responses will vary.

Week 17

Day 1
1. D
2. C
3. A
4. B
5. A

Day 2
1. B
2. D
3. C
4. B
5. C

Day 3
1. A
2. C
3. C
4. D
5. D

Day 4
1. A
2. B
3. C
4. A
5. A
6. B

ANSWER KEY *(cont.)*

Week 17 *(cont.)*

Day 5

Responses will vary.

Week 18

Day 1

1. C
2. B
3. D
4. B
5. A

Day 2

1. B
2. A
3. B
4. C
5. D

Day 3

1. B
2. A
3. B
4. A
5. B

Day 4

1. C
2. D
3. B
4. B
5. C
6. D

Day 5

Responses will vary.

Week 19

Day 1

1. A
2. B
3. C
4. D
5. A

Day 2

1. B
2. C
3. D
4. A
5. A

Day 3

1. B
2. D
3. C
4. A
5. A

Day 4

1. C
2. A
3. C
4. C
5. C
6. D

Day 5

Responses will vary.

Week 20

Day 1

1. B
2. D
3. B
4. A
5. B

Day 2

1. C
2. B
3. A
4. A
5. A

Day 3

1. B
2. A
3. B
4. C
5. B

Day 4

1. B
2. C
3. C
4. B
5. B
6. B

Day 5

Responses will vary.

Week 21

Day 1

1. D
2. D
3. C
4. B
5. C

Day 2

1. B
2. A
3. B
4. B
5. B

Day 3

1. B
2. D
3. A
4. B
5. D

Day 4

1. D
2. B
3. A
4. C
5. A
6. D

Day 5

Responses will vary.

Week 22

Day 1

1. C
2. D
3. A
4. B
5. A

Day 2

1. C
2. B
3. D
4. C
5. D

Day 3

1. B
2. B
3. C
4. D
5. D

Day 4

1. A
2. D
3. B
4. B
5. A
6. D

Day 5

Responses will vary.

Week 23

Day 1

1. D
2. A
3. D
4. B
5. D

Day 2

1. D
2. D
3. B
4. B
5. A

ANSWER KEY *(cont.)*

Week 23 *(cont.)*

Day 3

1. B
2. C
3. D
4. C
5. B

Day 4

1. D
2. B
3. C
4. B
5. C
6. C

Day 5

Responses will vary.

Week 24

Day 1

1. C
2. A
3. C
4. C
5. C

Day 2

1. A
2. D
3. C
4. B
5. C

Day 3

1. B
2. D
3. D
4. B
5. D

Day 4

1. D
2. B
3. D
4. D
5. B
6. C

Day 5

Responses will vary.

Week 25

Day 1

1. C
2. A
3. C
4. D
5. B

Day 2

1. D
2. B
3. C
4. D
5. A

Day 3

1. B
2. D
3. C
4. B
5. B

Day 4

1. A
2. A
3. A
4. C
5. A
6. B

Day 5

Responses will vary.

Week 26

Day 1

1. C
2. C
3. A
4. A
5. A

Day 2

1. C
2. C
3. C
4. B
5. A

Day 3

1. D
2. C
3. B
4. B
5. A

Day 4

1. B
2. A
3. B
4. D
5. A
6. C

Day 5

Responses will vary.

Week 27

Day 1

1. C
2. D
3. D
4. A
5. B

Day 2

1. D
2. D
3. B
4. A
5. A

Day 3

1. A
2. D
3. A
4. C
5. C

Day 4

1. D
2. D
3. C
4. B
5. A
6. C

Day 5

Responses will vary.

Week 28

Day 1

1. C
2. B
3. B
4. D
5. D

Day 2

1. A
2. C
3. D
4. C
5. B

Day 3

1. A
2. A
3. A
4. C
5. D

Day 4

1. B
2. A
3. D
4. D
5. C
6. A

Day 5

Responses will vary.

ANSWER KEY *(cont.)*

Week 29

Day 1
1. B
2. C
3. D
4. D
5. B

Day 2
1. B
2. D
3. C
4. A
5. C

Day 3
1. B
2. D
3. A
4. B
5. A

Day 4
1. D
2. A
3. C
4. A
5. A
6. B

Day 5
Responses will vary.

Week 30

Day 1
1. A
2. C
3. B
4. A
5. B

Day 2
1. D
2. B
3. B
4. B
5. B

Day 3
1. B
2. D
3. B
4. B
5. B

Day 4
1. A
2. D
3. B
4. D
5. D
6. C

Day 5
Responses will vary.

Week 31

Day 1
1. C
2. A
3. B
4. A
5. A

Day 2
1. B
2. A
3. A
4. C
5. D

Day 3
1. D
2. A
3. D
4. C
5. B

Day 4
1. D
2. A
3. A
4. C
5. A
6. D

Day 5
Responses will vary.

Week 32

Day 1
1. A
2. C
3. A
4. B
5. D

Day 2
1. A
2. D
3. A
4. A
5. A

Day 3
1. A
2. A
3. A
4. D
5. C

Day 4
1. C
2. A
3. D
4. C
5. C
6. B

Day 5
Responses will vary.

Week 33

Day 1
1. D
2. C
3. A
4. A
5. B

Day 2
1. D
2. D
3. C
4. C
5. C

Day 3
1. C
2. A
3. A
4. C
5. A

Day 4
1. B
2. C
3. A
4. A
5. C
6. D

Day 5
Responses will vary.

Week 34

Day 1
1. B
2. B
3. A
4. C
5. B

Day 2
1. B
2. B
3. A
4. D
5. A

Day 3
1. A
2. D
3. D
4. B
5. C

ANSWER KEY *(cont.)*

Week 34 *(cont.)*

Day 4
1. B
2. A
3. A
4. B
5. A
6. D

Day 5
Responses will vary.

Week 35

Day 1
1. C
2. C
3. A
4. D
5. B

Day 2
1. A
2. B
3. B
4. A
5. B

Day 3
1. D
2. A
3. B
4. C
5. D

Day 4
1. C
2. A
3. A
4. B
5. D
6. A

Day 5
Responses will vary.

Week 36

Day 1
1. A
2. C
3. C
4. A
5. A

Day 2
1. A
2. C
3. B
4. C
5. D

Day 3
1. C
2. A
3. B
4. A
5. D

Day 4
1. B
2. B
3. A
4. A
5. C
6. C

Day 5
Responses will vary.

REFERENCES CITED

Marzano, Robert. 2010. When Practice Makes Perfect...Sense. *Educational Leadership* 68 (3): 81–83.

National Reading Panel. 2000. Report of the National Reading Panel. *Teaching Children to Read: An Evidence-Based Assessment of the Scientific Research Literature on Reading and its Implication for Reading Instruction* (NIH Publication No. 00-4769). Washington, DC: U.S. Government Printing Office.

Rasinski, Timothy V. 2003. *The Fluent Reader: Oral Reading Strategies for Building Word Recognition, Fluency, and Comprehension*. New York: Scholastic.

———. 2006. Fluency: An Oft-Neglected Goal of the Reading Program. In *Understanding and Implementing Reading First Initiatives*, ed. C. Cummins, 60–71. Newark, DE: International Reading Association.

Wolf, Maryanne. 2005. *What is Fluency? Fluency Development: As the Bird Learns to Fly*. Scholastic professional paper. New York: ReadAbout. http://teacher.scholastic.com/products/fluencyformula/pdfs/What_is_Fluency.pdf (accessed June 8, 2007).

DIGITAL RESOURCES

Accessing the Digital Resources

The digital resources can be downloaded by following these steps:

1. Go to **www.tcmpub.com/digital**
2. Sign in or create an account.
3. Click **Redeem Content** and enter the ISBN number, located on page 2 and the back cover, into the appropriate field on the website.
4. Respond to the prompts using the book to view your account and available digital content.
5. Choose the digital resources you would like to download. You can download all the files at once, or you can download a specific group of files.

ISBN:
9781425809256

Please note: Some files provided for download have large file sizes. Download times for these larger files will vary based on your download speed.

CONTENTS OF THE DIGITAL RESOURCES

Teacher Resources

- Assessing Fluency
- Writing Rubric
- Practice Page Item Analysis Chart
- Student Item Analysis Chart

Student Resources

- Practice Pages

NOTES